Spelling and Vocabulary Skills

Level 5

Teacher's Annotated Edition

A Division of The McGraw·Hill Companies

Columbus, Ohio

www.sra4kids.com

SRA/McGraw-Hill

A Division of The McGraw·Hill Companies

2005 Imprint

Copyright © 2002 by SRA/McGraw-Hill.

Send all inquiries to:
SRA/McGraw-Hill
8787 Orion Place
Columbus, OH 43240-4027

Printed in the United States of America.

ISBN 0-07-571113-3

3 4 5 6 7 8 9 POH 07 06 05 04

Table of Contents

Unit 1 **Cooperation and Competition**

Lesson 1 *"Class President"*
Vocabulary: Discovering Word Meanings........................ 2
Spelling: The /a/ Sound.. 4

Lesson 2 *"The Marble Champ"*
Vocabulary: Context Clues 6
Spelling: The /e/ Sound.. 8

Lesson 3 *"Juggling"*
Vocabulary: Word Parts.. 10
Spelling: The /o/ and /aw/ Sounds 12

Lesson 4 *"The Abacus Contest"*
Vocabulary: Using the Dictionary............................... 14
Spelling: The /i/ Sound 16

Lesson 5 *"S.O.R. Losers"*
Vocabulary: Using the Thesaurus................................ 18
Spelling: The /u/ Sound... 20

Lesson 6 *"Founders of the Children's Rain Forest"*
Vocabulary: Word Mapping....................................... 22
Spelling: The Short-Vowel Sounds.............................. 24

Unit 2 **Astronomy**

Lesson 1 *"Galileo"*
Vocabulary: Science Words 26
Spelling: The /ā/ Sound 28

Lesson 2 *"Telescopes"*
Vocabulary: Greek Roots 30
Spelling: The /ē/ Sound... 32

Lesson 3 *"The Heavenly Zoo"*
Vocabulary: Homographs 34
Spelling: The /ē/ Sound... 36

Lesson 4 *"Circles, Squares, and Daggers:
How Native Americans Watched the Skies"*
Vocabulary: Latin Roots 38
Spelling: The /ō/ Sound... 40

Lesson 5 *"The Mystery of Mars"*
Vocabulary: Prefixes.. 42
Spelling: The /ī/ Sound 44

Lesson 6 *"Stars"*
Vocabulary: Suffixes 46
Spelling: The /o͞o/ and /ū/ Sounds 48

Lesson 7 *"The Book that Saved the Earth"*
Vocabulary: Review... 50
Spelling: The Long-Vowel Sounds 52

Unit 3　Heritage

Lesson 1　*"The Land I Lost: Adventures of a Boy in Vietnam"*
Vocabulary: Context Clues **54**
Spelling: The /ow/ Sound **56**

Lesson 2　*"In Two Worlds; A Yup'ik Eskimo Family"*
Vocabulary: Concept Words **58**
Spelling: The Final /əl/ Sound **60**

Lesson 3　*"The West Side"*
Vocabulary: Spanish Words. **62**
Spelling: The /or/ and /är/ Sounds **64**

Lesson 4　*"Love as Strong as Ginger"*
Vocabulary: Levels of Specificity **66**
Spelling: Consonant Blends **68**

Lesson 5　*"The Night Journey"*
Vocabulary: Antonyms **70**
Spelling: Silent Letters **72**

Lesson 6　*"Parmele"*
Vocabulary: Review. **74**
Spelling: Review **76**

Unit 4　Making a New Nation

Lesson 1　*". . . If You Lived at the Time of the American Revolution"*
Vocabulary: Social Studies Words **78**
Spelling: Plurals **80**

Lesson 2　*"The Night the Revolution Began"*
Vocabulary: Synonyms. **82**
Spelling: Possessive Nouns **84**

Lesson 3　*"The Midnight Ride of Paul Revere"*
Vocabulary: Figurative Language **86**
Spelling: Compound Words **88**

Lesson 4　*"The Declaration of Independence"*
Vocabulary: Base Word Families **90**
Spelling: Changing *y* to *i* **92**

Lesson 5　*"The Master Spy of Yorktown"*
Vocabulary: Words with Multiple Meanings. **94**
Spelling: Doubling Final Consonants **96**

Lesson 6　*"Shh! We're Writing the Constitution"*
Vocabulary: Word Origins. **98**
Spelling: Dropping *e* and Adding Endings. **100**

Lesson 7　*"We, the People of the United States"*
Vocabulary: Review. **102**
Spelling: Review **104**

Unit 5 **Going West**

Lesson I *"Sacagawea's Journey"*
Vocabulary: Concept Words 106
Spelling: Homophones 108

Lesson 2 *"Buffalo Hunt"*
Vocabulary: Synonyms. 110
Spelling: Words with *dis-* and *mis-* 112

Lesson 3 *"The Journal of Wong Ming-Chung"*
Vocabulary: Words with Multiple Meanings. 114
Spelling: Words with *-ent* and *-ant* 116

Lesson 4 *"The Coming of the Long Knives"*
Vocabulary: Foreign Words. 118
Spelling: Words with *-tion, -sion,* or *-sure* 120

Lesson 5 *"Old Yeller and the Bear"*
Vocabulary: Similes 122
Spelling: Words with *-ed* and *-ing* 124

Lesson 6 *"Bill Pickett: Rodeo-Ridin' Cowboy"*
Vocabulary: Compound Words 126
Spelling: Words with *-er* and *-est* 128

Lesson 7 *"McBroom the Rainmaker"*
Vocabulary: Review 130
Spelling: Review 132

Unit 6 **Journeys and Quests**

Lesson I *"The Story of Jumping Mouse"*
Vocabulary: Personification 134
Spelling: Greek Roots. 136

Lesson 2 *"Trapped by the Ice!"*
Vocabulary: Homophones 138
Spelling: Latin Roots 140

Lesson 3 *"Apollo 11: First Moon Landing"*
Vocabulary: Derivations 142
Spelling: Words of Spanish Origin 144

Lesson 4 *"When Shlemiel Went to Warsaw"*
Vocabulary: Multicultural Words 146
Spelling: Words of French Origin 148

Lesson 5 *"The Search"*
Vocabulary: Metaphor 150
Spelling: Other Foreign Words. 152

Lesson 6 *"Alberic the Wise"*
Vocabulary: Review 154
Spelling: Review 156

Vocabulary Rules 158

Spelling Strategies 161

Spelling Rules 163

UNIT I Cooperation and Competition • **Lesson I** *Class President*

Discovering Word Meanings

As you read "Class President," you may come across words you do not know. You can begin to discover the meanings of these words by asking yourself some questions. For example, the word *bore* in the sentence below from "Class President" may be unfamiliar, but you can ask yourself the following questions about the word.

▶ The principal, Mr. Herbertson, spoke in a loud voice and had eyes that seemed to **bore** right into your head when he looked at you.

1. **Have I seen this word before? Where?**

2. **Does the word look like any other word I know?**

3. **What can I tell from the words surrounding the word?**

 **Try It!** Write your responses to questions 1 and 2 for the word *bore*.

Answers will vary.
_____

_____

What can you tell from the other words surrounding the word? Write a definition for the word *bore*, based on what you already know about the word and how it is used in the sentence.

bore: **Answers will vary.**
_____

_____

UNIT I Cooperation and Competition • **Lesson I** *Class President*

▶ **Discovering Word Meanings**

Practice

Here are more words, along with *bore*, from "Class President" that may have unfamiliar meanings.

nomination   bore   second   move   campaign

Write the word from the list above that best completes each of the following sentences. Do not worry if you don't know the exact meaning of the word. Make your best guess based on what you already know about the word and how it could be used in a sentence.

1. I _____**move**_____ that the money from the fundraiser be

   used to feed the homeless.

2. Do you accept the Republican **nomination** for

   President?

3. As part of his **campaign** he visited steel factories

   and talked to the workers.

4. If you propose that we adjourn the meeting, I will

   _____**second**_____ that proposal.

5. We used an electric drill to _____**bore**_____ holes in the

   wood.

VOCABULARY

The /a/ Sound

Word List

1. cancel
2. travel
3. castle
4. salad
5. catalog
6. cabinet
7. blanket
8. tractor
9. magnet
10. cabin
11. palace
12. glance
13. paddle
14. sang
15. shampoo

Selection Words

16. accident
17. activity
18. classroom
19. absent
20. ballot

Pattern Study

The /a/ sound is always spelled with one *a* whether it appears at the beginning, middle, or end of a syllable.

▶ Write the spelling words with the /a/ sound at the beginning of a syllable.

1. accident   3. activity
2. absent

▶ Write the spelling words with the /a/ sound in the middle of a syllable.

4. cancel   13. salad
5. catalog   14. cabinet
6. blanket   15. tractor
7. magnet   16. palace
8. glance   17. paddle
9. sang   18. shampoo
10. classroom 19. ballot
11. travel   20. cabin
12. castle

UNIT 1 Cooperation and Competition • **Lesson 1** *Class President*

▶ **The /a/ Sound**

Strategies

Family Strategy **Write the spelling words on which these words are based.**

21. accidentally   accident

22. magnetic   magnet

23. glanced   glance

24. activities   activity

25. traveling   travel

Visualization Strategy **Write the spelling words by filling in the missing vowels.**

26. c__nc__l   cancel

27. c__stl__   castle

28. c__b__n__t   cabinet

29. s__ng   sang

30. __bs__nt   absent

31. sh__mpoo   shampoo

32. s__l__d   salad

33. c__b__n   cabin

34. b__ll__t   ballot

35. c__t__l__g   catalog

36. p__ddl__   paddle

37. tr__ct__r   tractor

38. p__l__c__   palace

39. bl__nk__t   blanket

40. cl__ssroom   classroom

SPELLING

UNIT I Cooperation and Competition • **Lesson 2** *The Marble Champ*

Context Clues

You don't always need a dictionary when you find a word you don't know. Often you can come up with a definition by looking at the word itself and at the scene or situation being described by the words around it. This strategy is called examining context clues.

Read the following sentences from "The Marble Champ," paying close attention to the underlined word. Answer the questions that follow to come up with a definition for the word.

"I'll never be good at sports," she <u>fumed</u> one rainy day as she lay on her bed gazing at the shelf her father had made to hold her awards. "I wish I could win something, anything, even marbles."

1. Try to sum up the idea or situation being described. What is going on in the paragraph?

   Lupe is upset because she has never won any awards for sports.

2. How is the word *fumed* being used? Is it an object? Is it being used to describe something? Is it something she does? Write whether *fumed* is a thing, a word to describe something, or an action word.

   The word *fumed* is something she does, or an action word.

3. Using these context clues, write a definition for *fumed*.

   spoke in an angry way

Context Clues

VOCABULARY

Practice

Read the following groups of sentences from "The Marble Champ" and use context clues to guess the meaning of each underlined word. Don't worry if the meaning you write is not exactly right. Just make your best guess and explain in the second space how you got your answer.

Example:

She hopped out of bed and <u>rummaged</u> through the closet until she found a can full of her brother's marbles.

Meaning: looked or searched

Explain: The word means something that the girl does to find a can of marbles.

4. She beat her first <u>opponent</u> easily, and felt sorry for the girl because she didn't have anyone to cheer for her. Except for her sack of marbles, she was all alone. Lupe invited the girl, whose name was Rachel, to stay with them. She smiled and said, "OK." The four of them walked to a card table in the middle of the outfield where Lupe was assigned another opponent.

Meaning: someone you play against

Explain: The opponent is the girl Rachel. Lupe plays marbles with Rachel and beats her.

5. He knew his daughter thought she was no good at sports and he wanted to encourage her. He even <u>rigged</u> some lights in the backyard so she could practice after dark.

Meaning: constructed

Explain: The word means something the father does to put up lights.

The /e/ Sound

Word List

1. sense
2. plenty
3. enemy
4. quest
5. wealth
6. sweater
7. feather
8. welcome
9. shelter
10. meant
11. edit
12. health
13. breath
14. tennis
15. swept

Selection Words

16. treasure
17. bedspread
18. chess
19. strengthen
20. shelf

Pattern Study

The **/e/ sound** can be spelled with one *e*, whether it is between two consonants or before a consonant. The /e/ sound can also be spelled with *ea*.

▶ Write the spelling words with the /e/ sound spelled *e*.

1. sense
2. swept
3. strengthen
4. plenty
5. tennis
6. shelf
7. welcome
8. quest
9. enemy
10. shelter
11. chess
12. edit

▶ Write the spelling words with the /e/ sound spelled *ea*.

13. meant
14. sweater
15. health
16. wealth
17. breath
18. treasure
19. feather

▶ Write the spelling word with the /e/ sound spelled with one *e* and with *ea*.

20. bedspread

▶ **The /e/ Sound**

SPELLING

Strategies

Rhyming Strategy Write the spelling word that rhymes with each of the following words.

21. twenty **plenty**

22. kept **swept**

23. tent **meant**

24. weather **feather**

25. zest **quest**

Proofreading Stategy Circle the spelling words that are spelled incorrectly in the following paragraph and write them correctly in the spaces provided.

There are many things we can do to maintain our (helth). One fun activity that can help us stay fit is playing (tenis). Unlike chess, which gives the brain a workout, tennis gets the heart going. After a long match, a glass of water and a chair are (wellcome) sights! Lifting weights also keeps us healthy because it can (strengthan) our muscles. It makes a lot of sense to make time for exercise. Our health is a (tresure) we should cherish.

26. **health**

27. **tennis**

28. **welcome**

29. **strengthen**

30. **treasure**

UNIT 1 Cooperation and Competition • **Lesson 3** *Juggling*

Word Parts

Exploring context clues is not the only strategy you can use to figure out the meaning of a word. Sometimes the clues are within the word itself. All you need to do is break the word into its parts and figure out what each part means.

 **Try It!** The underlined words in the following sentences are broken down into their parts. Write the meaning of each part. Then write a definition for the whole word.

1. <u>Racquetball</u> is played in a small, enclosed court.

   racquet: **an object with netting and a handle used to hit a ball**

   ball: **a round object used in sports**

   Definition: **a game that is played on a small court with a ball and a racquet**

2. Her bracelets jangled as they slid up and down her <u>forearm</u>.

   fore: **in front of**

   arm: **the part of the body between the shoulder and the wrist**

   Definition: **the front of the arm, between the elbow and the wrist**

3. His daughter is a <u>preteen</u> and is in the sixth grade.

   pre: **before**

   teen: **someone between the ages of 13 and 19**

   Definition: **someone who is not yet 13 years old**

▶ **Word Parts**

VOCABULARY

Practice

You may not know the meanings of the following words, but each one has a prefix, suffix, or base that you may be familiar with. After each word, write three words from the list with the same prefix, suffix, or base.

parallel	paraphrase	sensitive	paragraph
biology	ecology	geology	sensible
sensation			

4. paradigm

Write three words with the prefix ***para,*** which means *beside.*

parallel   paragraph

paraphrase

5. musicology

Write three words with the suffix ***ology,*** which means *study or science of.*

ecology   biology

geology

6. sensory

Write three words with the root ***sens,*** which means *feel.*

sensation   sensitive

sensible

The /o/ and /aw/ Sounds

Word List

1. thought
2. brought
3. congress
4. topic
5. fought
6. ought
7. promise
8. awful
9. proper
10. collar
11. cause
12. caught
13. comet
14. broad
15. common

Selection Words

16. volleyball
17. lockers
18. office
19. intercom
20. offered

Pattern Study

> **The /o/ sound** can be spelled with one *o*.
> **The /aw/ sound** can be spelled with *o*, *augh*, *aw*, *ough*, or *au*.

▶ Write the spelling words with the /o/ sound spelled *o*.

1. congress
2. promise
3. collar
4. comet
5. lockers
6. topic
7. proper
8. common
9. volleyball
10. intercom

▶ Write the spelling words with the /aw/ sound spelled *ough*.

11. ought
12. brought
13. fought
14. thought

▶ Write the spelling words with /aw/ spelled *aw* and *au*.

15. awful
16. cause

▶ Write the spelling word with /aw/ spelled *augh*.

17. caught

▶ Write the spelling words with /aw/ spelled *o*.

18. office
19. offered

Name _____   Date _____

UNIT I Cooperation and Competition • **Lesson 3** *Juggling*

▶ The /o/ and /aw/ Sounds

Strategies

Pronunciation Strategy Write the spelling words in the spaces that follow. Draw lines between each syllable.

20. con\gress
21. top\ic
22. prom\ise
23. prop\er
24. col\lar
25. com\mon
26. com\et
27. cause
28. broad
29. caught

30. aw\ful
31. ought
32. fought
33. brought
34. thought
35. vol\ley\ball
36. lock\ers
37. of\fice
38. in\ter\com
39. of\fered

Family Strategy Write the spelling words that are a different tense of the following words.

40. promised   promise
41. catch   caught
42. fight   fought
43. bring   brought
44. think   thought

SPELLING

UNIT 1 Cooperation and Competition • **Lesson 4** *The Abacus Contest*

Using the Dictionary

> You know that the dictionary is a place to go for the definition of a word. You may not realize, however, that you can find out many other things about a word from its entry in the dictionary.

 **Try It!** **Answer the following questions about this dictionary entry.**

ignite 1. To set on fire: *We ignited the sticks for the campfire with a match.* 2. To begin to burn; catch on fire: *You must be careful with how you store oily rags because they ignite easily.* **ig nite** \ig nīt'\ *verb*, **ignited, igniting**.

1. What are two definitions for *ignite?*

to set on fire

to begin to burn; catch on fire

2. What is one example sentence given for the word *ignite?*
Answers will vary.

3. Write the word *ignite* and put a line between the syllables.
ig|nite

4. Write the pronunciation for the word *ignite.* **\ig nīt'**

5. What is the part of speech of *ignite?* **verb**

6. What are two other words related to *ignite?*

ignited

igniting

Practice

Look at the following word entries from a dictionary and follow the instructions.

lagoon A shallow body of water usually connected to a larger body of water. **la goon** \lə gün'\ *noun, plural* **lagoons**.

7. What is the part of speech? <u>noun</u>

8. Break the word *lagoon* into syllables. <u>la|goon</u>

9. Write the pronunciation for *lagoon.* <u>lə gün'</u>

masterful 1. Tending to control; showing power: *I use a masterful voice when I give my dog a command.* 2. Having great skill or knowledge: *The singer gave a masterful performance.* **mas ter ful** \mas' tər fəl\ *adjective.* –**masterfully** *adverb.*

10. Write two definitions for the word *masterful.*
<u>tending to control; having great skill</u>
<u>or knowledge</u>

11. Write another related word. <u>masterfully</u>

12. What is the part of speech of *masterful?* <u>adjective</u>

VOCABULARY

UNIT I Cooperation and Competition • **Lesson 4** *The Abacus Contest*

The /i/ Sound

Word List

1. width
2. glimpse
3. twist
4. blizzard
5. lyrics
6. simple
7. built
8. system
9. igloo
10. mystery
11. limit
12. visit
13. imitate
14. whistle
15. thrift

Selection Words

16. mistake
17. giggled
18. quilt
19. begin
20. division

Pattern Study

The /i/ sound can be spelled with *i*, *y*, or *ui*.

▶ Write the spelling words with the /i/ sound spelled *i*.

1. width
2. twist
3. lyrics
4. igloo
5. visit
6. whistle
7. mistake
8. quilt
9. division
10. glimpse
11. blizzard
12. simple
13. limit
14. imitate
15. thrift
16. giggled
17. begin

▶ Write the spelling words with the /i/ sound spelled *y*.

18. system
19. mystery

▶ Write the spelling word with the /i/ sound spelled *ui*.

20. built

Strategies

Rhyming Strategy Write the spelling words that rhyme with the following words.

21. guilt ___built___   24. dimple ___simple___

22. insist ___twist___   25. thistle ___whistle___

23. gizzard ___blizzard___   26. shift ___thrift___

Family Strategy Write the spelling words that are related to the following words.

27. imitation ___imitate___   29. mistaken ___mistake___

28. beginning ___begin___   30. mysterious ___mystery___

Dictionary Strategy Words are listed in alphabetical order in the dictionary. When placing words in alphabetical order, you will sometimes have to look at the second, third, or fourth letter of each word. Put the spelling words from the Word List in alphabetical order.

31. ___blizzard___   39. ___simple___

32. ___built___   40. ___system___

33. ___glimpse___   41. ___thrift___

34. ___igloo___   42. ___twist___

35. ___imitate___   43. ___visit___

36. ___limit___   44. ___whistle___

37. ___lyrics___   45. ___width___

38. ___mystery___

SPELLING

Using the Thesaurus

As you know, the dictionary explains the meaning of a word, usually in the form of a phrase. A thesaurus contains synonyms for a word, single words that mean generally the same thing. A thesaurus is a good tool for finding word meanings. Just make sure you identify the correct synonym based on context clues.

Read the following sentences from "S.O.R. Losers," paying close attention to the underlined word. Then choose a synonym from the thesaurus entry that best replaces the underlined word.

1. "Why? We're good at other things. Why can't we <u>stick</u> with that?"

   stick, *n.* — *Syn.* branch, limb, stem, bough, twig . . .
   stick, *v.* — *Syn.* 1. pierce, spear, stab, puncture . . . 2. fasten, glue, attach, paste . . . 3. hold, stay, hang on to, follow . . .

   A synonym for *stick* would be **Answers will vary.** .

2. "Don't be so smart," he returned. "I'm trying to be supportive."
   "I'm sick of <u>support</u>!" I yelled and left the room.

   support, *v.* — *Syn.* 1. hold up, uphold, bear, carry, strengthen . . .
   2. maintain, nurture, nourish, care for . . .
   support, *n.* — *Syn.* 1. approval, encouragement, aid . . .
   2. foundation, groundwork, base, prop . . .

   A synonym for *support* would be **Answers will vary.** .

UNIT I Cooperation and Competition • **Lesson 5** *S.O.R. Losers*

▶ **Using the Thesaurus**

Practice

Replace the underlined words from "S.O.R. Losers" with synonyms from a thesaurus. Be sure to read the whole sentence or paragraph. Context clues will help you decide which synonyms to choose.

3. NEWSPAPER: Do you want to win?
ME: Wouldn't mind knowing what it feels like. For the
<u>novelty</u>.
Answers will vary. _____

4. One by one she called our names. Each time one of us
went up, looking like <u>cringing</u> but grinning worms, there
was some general craziness . . .
Answers will vary. _____

5. "Right," said Radosh. "It's not like we're committing
<u>treason</u> or something. People have a right to be losers."
Answers will vary. _____

6. "I'm sick and tired of people telling me we have to win,"
said Root.
"I think my folks are getting ready to <u>disown</u> me," said
Hays.
Answers will vary. _____

7. Ed is no jock and neither are his friends. Playing a sport is
sure to mean only one thing for them—total <u>humiliation</u>.
Answers will vary. _____

VOCABULARY

UNIT 1 Cooperation and Competition • **Lesson 5** *S.O.R. Losers*

The /u/ Sound

Word List

1. study
2. clumsy
3. money
4. trouble
5. trumpet
6. country
7. honey
8. chuckle
9. hunger
10. none
11. struggle
12. bulb
13. thunder
14. bundle
15. mutter

Selection Words

16. support
17. hundred
18. done
19. supposed
20. something

Pattern Study

The **/u/ sound** can be spelled with *u, o_e,* or *ou.*

▶ Write the spelling words with the /u/ sound spelled *u.*

1. study
2. trumpet
3. bundle
4. mutter
5. thunder
6. support
7. supposed
8. clumsy
9. hunger
10. struggle
11. chuckle
12. bulb
13. hundred

▶ Write the spelling words with the /u/ sound spelled *o_e.*

14. none
15. honey
16. something
17. money
18. done

▶ Write the spelling words with the /u/ sound spelled *ou.*

19. trouble
20. country

▶ **The /u/ Sound**

SPELLING

Strategies

Meaning Strategy Write the spelling words that belong with each group of synonyms.

21. awkward, stumbling   **clumsy** _____

22. bunch, package   **bundle** _____

23. finished, over   **done** _____

24. fight, strive   **struggle** _____

25. mumble, murmur   **mutter** _____

Proofreading Strategy Circle the spelling words in the following sentences that are misspelled and write them correctly on the spaces provided. If the words are spelled correctly, leave the line blank.

26. My little sister learned to count to one (hondred.)

    hundred _____

27. Mexico is a (contry) that borders the United States.

    country _____

28. He likes to use (hunny) instead of sugar to sweeten his tea.

    honey _____

29. The car started right away and we were able to get to school without any trouble.

    _____

30. I could tell that Julio was hiding (somthing) behind his back.

    something _____

Word Mapping

To make a map of a word, write the word in the center of your paper and brainstorm any word you can think of that is related. List these words on the bottom of your paper.

Once you have brainstormed, think of how you could put all your words into categories. Write these categories around the word and draw lines connecting them to that word. Then arrange the words from the bottom of the page under their categories on the word map.

Try mapping with the word *biologist* from "Founders of the Children's Rain Forest." Write the words from the list at the bottom of the page that go under each category. Then draw a line from the word *biologist* to each group of words.

Category: Animals studied

1. jaguar
2. macaw
3. ocelot

Category: Other scientists

4. botanist
5. zoologist
6. marine biologist

biologist

Category: Equipment

7. microscope
8. camera
9. slides

Category: Subjects studied

10. extinction
11. species
12. habitat

Words related to *biologist:* extinction, microscope, jaguar, species, botanist, zoologist, macaw, camera, ocelot, habitat, marine biologist, slides

▶ **Word Mapping**

Practice

Choose five words from your word map of *biologist*. Check the definitions of these words in a dictionary or thesaurus. Use these words in a sentence to show you know the meanings of each word. Be creative!

13. Answers will vary.

_____

_____

14. Answers will vary.

_____

_____

15. Answers will vary.

_____

_____

16. Answers will vary.

_____

_____

17. Answers will vary.

_____

_____

VOCABULARY

The Short-Vowel Sounds

Word List

1. jazz
2. double
3. taught
4. glove
5. leather
6. pansy
7. strict
8. prompt
9. bumblebee
10. taxi
11. pause
12. bought
13. myth
14. freckle
15. guilt

Selection Words

16. minute
17. pasture
18. rabbit
19. jungle
20. tropical

Pattern Study

As you have learned, the **short vowels** /a/, /e/, /o/, /aw/, /i/, and /u/ can be spelled in a variety of ways.

Test your knowledge of short-vowel spelling patterns by writing the appropriate spelling words under the correct vowel sound. After each word, write the letter or letters that spell that short-vowel sound.

▶ /e/

1. freckle   e   2. leather   ea

▶ /o/ and /aw/

3. taught   augh   6. prompt   o

4. bought   ough   7. pause   au

5. tropical   o

▶ /i/

8. guilt   ui   10. myth   y

9. strict   i   11. minute   i

▶ /u/

12. glove   o_e   14. bumblebee   u

13. double   ou   15. jungle   u

► **The Short-Vowel Sounds**

SPELLING

Strategies

Family Strategy Write the spelling words that belong in the same base word family as the words below.

16. mythical   myth
17. promptly   prompt
18. guilty   guilt
19. pansies   pansy
20. strictness   strict
21. gloved   glove

Rhyming Strategy Write the spelling words that rhyme with the words below.

22. caught   taught
23. heather   leather
24. built   guilt
25. above   glove
26. trouble   double
27. bungle   jungle
28. cause   pause
29. predict   strict
30. sought   bought

UNIT 2 Astronomy • **Lesson I** *Galileo*

Science Words

When you read about a new and challenging topic like astronomy, you may feel a little overwhelmed by all the new science words you find. Science seems to have its own language, and understanding what you read can be tough! Word mapping can help you make connections between these new words and the ones you might already know.

Meteorology involves the study of weather. Think of all the words you know that have to do with weather and Earth's atmosphere. Write them in the blanks around the word *meteorology* to create a science word map.

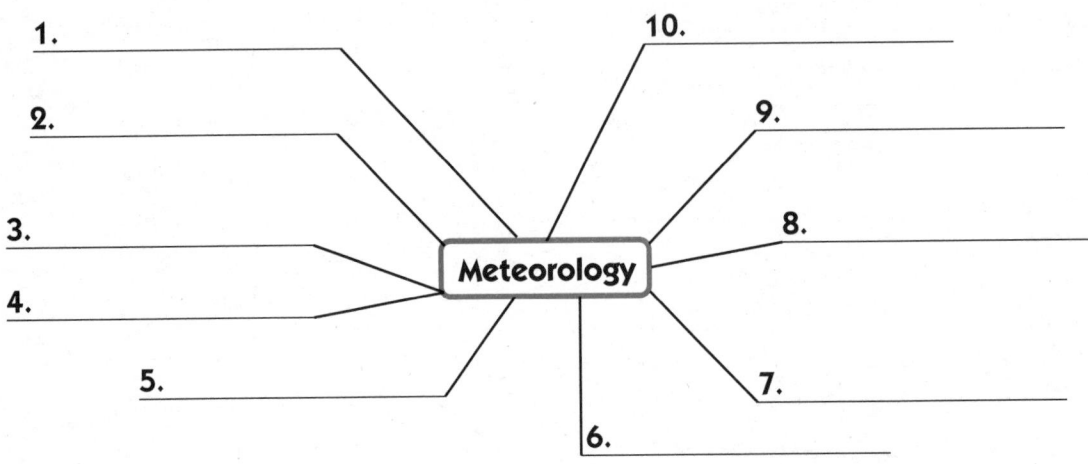

Name _____ Date _____

Practice

The words underlined in the following sentences are often used in the science of astronomy. Figure out the meaning of each word based on context clues. Then write your own sentences containing each word.

You may think that Earth is the only planet to have a <u>satellite</u>, or a heavenly body that moves around a larger body, but moons <u>orbit</u> other planets as well. When a moon orbits a planet, it moves in a circle around that planet. Neptune has a moon called Triton. Triton orbits Neptune in a <u>retrograde</u> motion: it travels around Neptune in the direction opposite the direction Neptune spins. Scientists were excited to discover this moon—as excited as they were to discover a <u>nova</u>, a star that suddenly becomes bright and then fades.

11. satellite: Answers will vary. _____

_____

12. orbit: Answers will vary. _____

_____

13. retrograde: Answers will vary. _____

_____

14. nova: Answers will vary. _____

_____

VOCABULARY

UNIT 2 Astronomy • **Lesson I** *Galileo*

The /ā/ Sound

Word List

1. scrape
2. favor
3. danger
4. sleigh
5. reins
6. layer
7. great
8. hasty
9. explain
10. daily
11. eight
12. straight
13. stale
14. neighbor
15. praise

Selection Words

16. sailors
17. wavy
18. crazy
19. amazed
20. bathed

Pattern Study

The /ā/ sound is most often spelled with *a*, *a_e*, *ai*, and *ay*, but can also be spelled with *ea*, *ei*, and *eigh*.

▶ Write the spelling words with the /ā/ sound spelled *a*.

1. favor
2. danger
3. hasty
4. wavy
5. crazy

▶ Write the spelling words with the /ā/ sound spelled *a_e*.

6. scrape
7. amazed
8. bathed
9. stale

▶ Write the spelling words with the /ā/ sound spelled *ai*.

10. praise
11. daily
12. straight
13. explain
14. sailors

▶ Write the spelling words with the /ā/ sound spelled *eigh*.

15. sleigh
16. neighbor
17. eight

▶ Write the spelling words with the /ā/ sound spelled *ea* and *ei*.

18. great
19. reins

The /ā/ Sound • Spelling and Vocabulary Skills

Name _____ Date _____

▶ **The /ā/ Sound**

Strategies

SPELLING

Meaning Strategy Homophones are words that sound the same, but are spelled differently and have different meanings. Fill in the blank in each of the following sentences with the correct homophone.

20. She received much ____**praise**____ from her parents.
praise/prays

21. The old woman ____**prays**____ every day in the chapel.
praise/prays

22. An arrow must be perfectly ____**straight**____ to be accurate.
strait/straight

23. A ____**strait**____ connects two large bodies of water.
strait/straight

24. We studied the ____**great**____ rulers of Europe in history class. **grate/great**

25. Be careful when you ____**grate**____ the cheese.
grate/great

26. Tighten your grip on the ____**reins**____ to control the horse. **reins/rains**

27. When it ____**rains**____ in the spring, new grass appears.
reins/rains

Visualization Strategy Fill in the missing vowels and write the spelling words.

28. f__vor ____**favor**____   32. n____ghbor ____**neighbor**____

29. sl____gh ____**sleigh**____   33. d____ly ____**daily**____

30. l__yer ____**layer**____   34. st__le ____**stale**____

31. s____lors ____**sailors**____   35. am__zed ____**amazed**____

UNIT 2   Astronomy • **Lesson 2** *Telescopes*

Greek Roots

Greek roots and roots from other languages are everywhere in our language. When you know the meaning of a root, you can figure out the meanings of many words that contain that root.

 **Try It!**   You may be familiar with the Greek root *tele* from words such as *telephone* and *television*. The following words also contain the root *tele*. Find a definition for each word in the dictionary and write it in the space provided.

1. televise: **Answers will vary.**

_____

2. telegraph: **Answers will vary.**

_____

3. telephoto lens: **Answers will vary.**

_____

4. teletypewriter: **Answers will vary.**

_____

5. telescope: **Answers will vary.**

_____

What do you think the root *tele* means?   **far away**

UNIT 2   Astronomy • **Lesson 2** *Telescopes*

Practice

The Greek root *cycl* means "circle." Below are five words that contain the Greek root *cycl*. Use each word in a sentence.

6. bicycle: **Answers will vary.**

_____

7. cyclone: **Answers will vary.**

_____

8. cycle: **Answers will vary.**

_____

9. encyclopedia: **Answers will vary.**

_____

10. cycling: **Answers will vary.**

_____

_____

VOCABULARY

UNIT 2 Astronomy • **Lesson 2** *Telescopes*

The /ē/ Sound

Word List

1. steep
2. decide
3. complete
4. reindeer
5. feature
6. freeze
7. beaver
8. sleeves
9. screen
10. scene
11. repeat
12. leader
13. beneath
14. appear
15. needle

Selection Words

16. peer
17. degree
18. previous
19. reduce
20. sequence

Pattern Study

Four spellings for **the /ē/ sound** are *e*, *e_e*, *ee*, and *ea*. The *e* and *e_e* spelling patterns are the most common.

▶ Write the spelling words with the /ē/ sound spelled *e*.

1. decide
2. previous
3. reduce
4. sequence

▶ Write the spelling words with the /ē/ sound spelled *e_e*.

5. scene
6. complete

▶ Write the spelling words with the /ē/ sound spelled *ee*.

7. steep
8. sleeves
9. needle
10. screen
11. reindeer
12. freeze
13. peer
14. degree

▶ Write the spelling words with the /ē/ sound spelled *ea*.

15. beaver
16. repeat
17. appear
18. beneath
19. leader
20. feature

UNIT 2 Astronomy • **Lesson 2** *Telescopes*

> ▶ The /ē/ Sound

Strategies

Family Strategy Write the spelling words that are related to the following words.

21. decision _____ **decide** _____   25. completion _____ **complete** _____

22. reduction _____ **reduce** _____   26. freezing _____ **freeze** _____

23. scenic _____ **scene** _____   27. sequentially _____ **sequence** _____

24. appearance _____ **appear** _____   28. peered _____ **peer** _____

Meaning Strategy Write the spelling words that are antonyms (opposites) of the following words.

29. over _____ **beneath** _____   32. next _____ **previous** _____

30. follower _____ **leader** _____   33. thaw _____ **freeze** _____

31. increase _____ **reduce** _____   34. unfinished _____ **complete** _____

Write the spelling words that are synonyms (have similar meanings) of the following words.

35. choose _____ **decide** _____   38. place _____ **scene** _____

36. look _____ **peer** _____   39. seem _____ **appear** _____

37. characteristic _____ **feature** _____   40. do again _____ **repeat** _____

SPELLING

UNIT 2 Astronomy • **Lesson 3** *The Heavenly Zoo*

Homographs

Homographs are words that are spelled the same but have different meanings and pronunciations. Often homographs will be pronounced differently by putting the stress on different syllables. Homographs are frequently different parts of speech as well. One might be a noun and another might be a verb.

The following passage from "The Heavenly Zoo" contains two homographs.

Now besides Yudistira, who was the eldest, the brothers were Sahadeva the all-wise, who was <u>learned</u> beyond all other men; Nakula the all-handsome, famed for his grace and beauty; Arjuna the all-powerful, who had never been defeated in any <u>contest</u> of arms . . .

Write a definition for the adjective *learned* and the noun *contest* based on how each is used in the passage above.

1. learned: **having or showing knowledge**
   _____

2. contest: **a competition or game**
   _____

Now write definitions from the dictionary for the verbs *learned* and *contest*.

3. learned: **came to know through study and practice**
   _____

4. contest: **to argue against**
   _____

UNIT 2 Astronomy • **Lesson 3** *The Heavenly Zoo*

▶ **Homographs**

VOCABULARY

Practice

The following sentence pairs contain homographs that are broken into syllables. Circle the syllable that should be stressed to make the word the correct homograph. Then write whether each homograph is a noun, verb, or adjective on the line after the sentence.

5. The president will ad (dress) the people on television.
   verb

   My (ad) dress will change when I move into a new house.
   noun

6. We were con (tent) to lie on the beach all day. **adjective**

   The paragraph is written correctly, but the (con) tent could be better. **noun**

7. The (des) ert is a dry place with miles of sand. **noun**

   The crew decided to des (ert) the ship when it began to sink.
   verb

8. He would set the tape player to re (cord) his favorite radio program. **verb**

   Be careful not to scratch that (rec) ord when you play it.
   noun

UNIT 2 Astronomy • **Lesson 3** *The Heavenly Zoo*

The /ē/ Sound

Word List

1. brief
2. grieve
3. nasty
4. receive
5. memory
6. scary
7. gasoline
8. piece
9. ceiling
10. ski
11. chief
12. belief
13. monkey
14. field
15. every

Selection Words

16. shield
17. journey
18. seized
19. story
20. safety

Pattern Study

The /ē/ sound can be spelled with *y*, *ey*, *ie*, *ei*, and *i*. Of these spelling patterns, *y* is the most common.

▶ Write the spelling words with the /ē/ sound spelled *y* or *ey*.

1. nasty   5. every
2. memory   6. journey
3. scary   7. safety
4. monkey   8. story

▶ Write the spelling words with the /ē/ sound spelled *ie*.

9. brief   13. belief
10. grieve   14. field
11. piece   15. shield
12. chief

▶ Write the spelling words with the /ē/ sound spelled *ei*.

16. receive   18. seized
17. ceiling

▶ Write the spelling word with the /ē/ sound spelled *i*.

19. ski

UNIT 2 Astronomy • **Lesson 3** *The Heavenly Zoo*

▶ **The /ē/ Sound**

Strategies

Visualization Strategy Fill in the missing vowels and
write the following spelling words.

20. gr__ __ve   **grieve** _____
21. s__ __zed   **seized** _____
22. sh__ __ld   **shield** _____
23. stor__   **story** _____
24. bel__ __f   **belief** _____
25. rec__ __ve   **receive** _____
26. p__ __ce   **piece** _____
27. c__ __ling   **ceiling** _____
28. f__ __ld   **field** _____
29. ch__ __f   **chief** _____

SPELLING

UNIT 2 Astronomy • **Lesson 4** *Circles, Squares, and Daggers*

Latin Roots

Latin roots are found in the English language even more often than Greek roots. Recognizing and knowing Latin roots can help you discover word meanings.

You may be familiar with the Latin root *vert*, which you can find in words such as *reverse* and *vertical*. In the dictionary, find the definitions for the following words containing *vert* and write the definitions next to each word.

1. convert: Answers will vary. The word means to turn around or transform.

2. extrovert: Answers will vary. The word means a person concerned with things outside him- or herself.

3. versatile: Answers will vary. The word means capable of changing.

4. divert: Answers will vary. The word means to turn aside.

5. vertigo: Answers will vary. The word means a state in which a person becomes dizzy.

6. What do you think the Latin root *vert* means? to turn

▶ **Latin Roots**

Practice

The following groups of words all have the same Latin roots. Circle the root that each word has in common. Then examine each word carefully and think of its definition. You may need to look up some words in a dictionary or thesaurus. Think about what the definitions have in common. Then write what you think each root means.

7. structure, reconstruction, destruction, instruct

The Latin root is *struct*. What does *struct* mean? **to build**

8. tribute, contribute, tributary, attribute

The Latin root is *trib*. What does *trib* mean? **to give**

9. reflex, flexible, flexor

The Latin root is *flex*. What does *flex* mean? **bend**

10. dentist, dental, dentistry

The Latin root is *dent*. What does *dent* mean? **tooth**

VOCABULARY

Name _____ Date _____

The /ō/ Sound

Word List

1. dome
2. boast
3. flown
4. overgrown
5. motor
6. postpone
7. hotel
8. quote
9. mostly
10. lifeboat
11. growth
12. robot
13. float
14. chosen
15. locate

Selection Words

16. social
17. spokes
18. shone
19. Mexico
20. adobe

Pattern Study

The /ō/ sound can be spelled with o, o_e, oa, and ow.

▶ Write the spelling words with the /ō/ sound in the accented syllable spelled o.

1. motor
2. hotel
3. mostly
4. robot
5. chosen
6. locate
7. Mexico
8. social
9. adobe

▶ Write the spelling words with the /ō/ sound spelled o_e.

10. dome
11. postpone
12. quote
13. spokes
14. shone

▶ Write the spelling words with the /ō/ sound spelled oa.

15. boast
16. lifeboat
17. float

▶ Write the spelling words with the /ō/ sound spelled ow.

18. flown
19. overgrown
20. growth

▶ **The /ō/ Sound**

SPELLING

Strategies

Visualization Strategy **Fill in the missing vowels and write the spelling words.**

21. fl__ __t   **float** _____
22. sh__n__   **shone** _____
23. s__cial   **social** _____
24. ad__be   **adobe** _____
25. ch__sen   **chosen** _____

26. b__ __ __st   **boast** _____
27. qu__t__   **quote** _____
28. p__stp__n__   **postpone** _____
29. l__cate   **locate** _____
30. sp__k__s   **spokes** _____

Proofreading Strategy **Circle the misspelled words in the following paragraph and write them correctly on the lines that follow.**

Our Trip to (Mexeco)

Last summer my parents and I took a trip to Cancun, Mexico. I had flown before, so I wasn't nervous when we drove to the airport. But there was a thunderstorm, and the airline had to (postpon) our flight. When we finally got to Cancun, our (hotle) was easy to locate. My parents had chosen a room with a great view of the water. The sun (shon) brightly each day, and when I wasn't on the beach I would (floate) in the pool.

31. **Mexico** _____
32. **postpone** _____
33. **hotel** _____
34. **shone** _____
35. **float** _____

Name _____ Date _____

Prefixes

As you read and learn new words, you will find many prefixes, or units of meaning at the beginnings of words. A prefix usually has the same meaning, no matter where you find it. If you can remember the meanings of prefixes, you can discover the meanings of words that contain them.

 **Try It!** Look at the word *microscopic* from the selection "The Mystery of Mars." It contains the prefix *micro-*. List five other words you know with the prefix *micro-*. You may use the dictionary if you cannot think of five words.

1. Answers will vary.
2. Answers will vary.
3. Answers will vary.
4. Answers will vary.
5. Answers will vary.

If you do not already know the meanings of some of your words, find the definitions in the dictionary.

Now that you know five words with the prefix *micro-,* what do you think it means? **small**

Write a definition for the word *microscopic*. Make your best guess based on what you know about the prefix and other words you may have seen before.

microscopic: **unable to be seen without the use of a microscope; very small**

UNIT 2 Astronomy • **Lesson 5** *The Mystery of Mars*

▶ **Prefixes**

Practice

Every number, from one to ten, has its own prefix. For example, in the word *bicycle*, the prefix *bi-*, meaning "two," tells you that a bicycle has two wheels. Study the following number prefixes.

uni = one	*bi* = two	*tri* = three
quad = four	*pent* = five	*hex* = six
hept = seven	*oct* = eight	*non* = nine
dec = ten		

Write the answers to the following riddles about number prefixes.

6. If a <u>hex</u>agon is a shape with six sides, what is a shape with five sides? __pentagon__

7. What is a vehicle with three wheels you might see a young child ride? __tricycle__

8. A <u>tri</u>athlon is an athletic contest with three events. How many events are in a <u>dec</u>athlon? __ten__

9. A <u>quar</u>tet is a musical group of four. What is a group of eight called? __octet__

10. <u>Tri</u>focal lenses are divided into three parts. What kind of lens has two parts? __bifocal__

UNIT 2 Astronomy • **Lesson 5** *The Mystery of Mars*

The /ī/ Sound

Word List

1. tiger
2. skyline
3. stride
4. lightning
5. idea
6. climate
7. recite
8. highlight
9. silent
10. design
11. excite
12. describe
13. style
14. cycle
15. deny

Selection Words

16. surprise
17. survive
18. entire
19. overnight
20. site

Pattern Study

The /ī/ sound can be spelled with i, i_e, y, and igh.

▶ Write the spelling words with the /ī/ sound spelled i.

1. tiger
2. idea
3. climate
4. silent
5. design

▶ Write the spelling words with the /ī/ sound spelled i_e.

6. stride
7. recite
8. excite
9. describe
10. surprise
11. survive
12. entire
13. site

▶ Write the spelling words with the /ī/ sound spelled y.

14. skyline
15. style
16. cycle
17. deny

▶ Write the spelling words with the /ī/ sound spelled igh.

18. lightning
19. highlight
20. overnight

The /ī/ Sound

SPELLING

Strategies

Meaning Strategy Write the spelling words that are antonyms of the following words.

21. noisy   silent
22. bore   excite
23. die   survive
24. none   entire
25. stand still stride

Dictionary Strategy Put the spelling words from the Word List in alphabetical order on the lines below. You may have to look at the second or third letter of a word to put it in order.

26. climate   34. lightning
27. cycle   35. recite
28. deny   36. silent
29. describe   37. skyline
30. design   38. stride
31. excite   39. style
32. highlight   40. tiger
33. idea

UNIT 2   Astronomy • **Lesson 6** *Stars*

Suffixes

Suffixes are units of meaning found at the ends of words.
Adding different suffixes to the same root word will give you
words with different meanings and different parts of speech.
For example, when you add **-ness** to a word such as *sad*, you
will have *sadness*, a noun. When you add **-ly** to the word *sad*,
you have the word *sadly*, which is an adverb.

 **Try It!**   **The underlined words in the first
sentences contain suffixes. Add the same
suffix to the base word underlined in the
second sentence and write the new word
in the blank.**

1. A <u>pianist</u> is one who plays the piano. A person who plays

   the <u>guitar</u> is called a ____**guitarist**____.

2. A <u>servant</u> is someone who serves another person. Someone

   who <u>assists</u> another person is an ____**assistant**____.

3. <u>Amusement</u> is the state of being amused. The state of being

   <u>amazed</u> is ____**amazement**____.

4. If a person is <u>childlike</u>, he or she resembles a child. If a

   place resembles a <u>home</u>, it is ____**homelike**____.

5. To <u>strengthen</u> is to make something strong.

   To ____**weaken**____ is to make something <u>weak</u>.

UNIT 2 Astronomy • **Lesson 6** *Stars*

▶ **Suffixes**

Practice

Add each of the following suffixes to the base word to create a noun, verb, adjective, or adverb, and write the new word in the blank to complete each sentence.

Add a suffix to *bright* to complete each sentence.

-ly   -ness   -en

6. noun: The ___**brightness**___ of the moon that night was amazing.

7. verb: Open the shades to ___**brighten**___ this dark room.

8. adverb: The car's headlights shone ___**brightly**___ on the dark road.

Add a suffix to *beauty* to complete each sentence.

-fully   -ful   -fy

9. verb: Some new flower beds will ___**beautify**___ the neighborhood.

10. adverb: They painted the new house ___**beautifully**___.

11. adjective: It was such a ___**beautiful**___ day, we decided to eat outside.

Add a suffix to *fear* to complete each sentence.

-ful   -less

12. adjective: We were ___**fearful**___ that the angry bees would attack us.

13. adjective: The race car driver is ___**fearless**___ and doesn't mind driving at any speed.

VOCABULARY

Name _____ Date _____

The /o͞o/ and /u͞/ Sounds

Word List

1. soup
2. music
3. clue
4. truth
5. bloom
6. lunar
7. toothbrush
8. cruise
9. smooth
10. cube
11. rooster
12. tissue
13. cartoon
14. duty
15. unite

Selection Words

16. future
17. group
18. unusual
19. universe
20. Pluto

Pattern Study

The /o͞o/ sound can be spelled *ou, o_e, _ue, u,* and *oo.* **The /u͞/ sound** can be spelled *u* and *u_e.*

▶ Write the spelling words with the /o͞o/ sound spelled *ou.*

1. group
2. soup

▶ Write the spelling words with the /o͞o/ sound spelled *oo.*

3. bloom
4. toothbrush
5. smooth
6. rooster
7. cartoon

▶ Write the spelling words with the /o͞o/ sound spelled *u.*

8. Pluto
9. truth
10. lunar
11. duty

▶ Write the spelling words with the /o͞o/ sound spelled *_ue.*

12. clue
13. tissue

▶ Write the spelling words with the /u͞/ sound spelled *u.*

14. future
15. unusual
16. universe
17. music
18. unite
19. cube

Name _____ Date _____

► The /o͞o/ and /ū/ Sounds

Strategies

Dictionary Strategy Some words do not appear as entry words in the dictionary. Write the spelling words you would look up to find the following words.

20. clues   **clue**

21. blooming   **bloom**

22. duties   **duty**

23. uniting   **unite**

24. futureless **future**

25. smoothed   **smooth**

26. cruising   **cruise**

27. cubed   **cube**

Meaning Strategy Fill in the blanks with the correct spelling words.

28. A ____**lunar**____ eclipse can cause the moon to appear red.

29. It is not ____**unusual**____ to find children on the playground at this hour.

30. We cannot even imagine the size of the ____**universe**____.

31. We can't dance until the ____**music**____ starts again.

32. ____**Pluto**____ is the planet farthest from the sun.

SPELLING

UNIT 2 Astronomy • **Lesson 7** *The Book that Saved the Earth*

► Review

When you know the meanings of roots, prefixes, and suffixes, you will find that discovering the meanings of new words is much easier. Use your knowledge of word parts, along with context clues, to tackle words you first thought were unfamiliar.

The following passages are from "The Book that Saved the Earth." As you read the passages, pay careful attention to the underlined word. Write what you think the meaning of that word is, based on context clues and what you know about the word parts. Check your answers in a dictionary.

1. **Historian:** Good afternoon. Welcome to our Museum of Ancient History, and to my department—curiosities of the good old, far-off twentieth century.

    historian: **Answers will vary.** _____

2. **Noodle** (Bowing): O Great and Mighty Think-Tank, most powerful and intelligent creature in the whole universe, what are your orders?
    Think-Tank (Peevishly): You left out part of my salutation, Apprentice Noodle. Go over the whole thing again.
    Noodle: It shall be done, sir. (In singsong) O Great and Mighty Think-Tank, Ruler of Macron and her two moons, most powerful . . .

    salutation: **Answers will vary.** _____

3. He opens his mouth wide. Omega and Iota watch him breathlessly. He bites down on corner of book, and pantomimes chewing and swallowing while making terrible faces.

    pantomimes: **Answers will vary.** _____

UNIT 2 Astronomy • **Lesson 7** *The Book that Saved the Earth*

Practice

Now, take the underlined words you defined on the previous page and use each one in a sentence that shows the word's meaning.

4. historian: **Answers will vary.**

_____

_____

5. salutation: **Answers will vary.**

_____

_____

6. pantomimes: **Answers will vary.**

_____

_____

VOCABULARY

UNIT 2 Astronomy • **Lesson 7** *The Book that Saved the Earth*

The Long-Vowel Sounds

Word List

1. prove
2. career
3. suit
4. area
5. iris
6. bowl
7. soothing
8. daydream
9. continue
10. type
11. nature
12. complain
13. spoken
14. weary
15. claim

Selection Words

16. humor
17. easel
18. diet
19. noble
20. realize

Pattern Study

The long-vowel sounds /ā/, /ē/, /ō/, /ī/, /o͞o/, and /ū/ can be spelled in a variety of ways.

▶ Write the spelling words that contain each long-vowel sound. After each word, write the long-vowel spelling pattern.

▶ /ā/

1. nature   a
2. complain   ai
3. daydream ay
4. claim   ai

▶ /ē/

5. area   e
6. career   ee
7. easel   ea
8. weary   ea
9. realize   e

▶ /ō/

10. bowl   ow
11. noble   o
12. spoken   o

▶ /ī/

13. iris   i
14. diet   i
15. type   y

UNIT 2 Astronomy • **Lesson 7** *The Book that Saved the Earth*

The Long-Vowel Sounds

Practice

Proofreading Strategy Circle the ten misspelled words in the following paragraph and write them correctly in the spaces provided.

If I could have any (carere) I wanted, I think I would choose to be an artist. I don't want a job where I'd have to sit in an office all day and wear a (suite). I would grow (weery) of that kind of life and would probably complain a lot. If I were an artist, I could take my (easle) into a garden and paint an (irys). I'd be sure to get in a daydream or two while I was at it! It would also be fun and quite (sooothing) to make a (bowle) out of spinning, wet clay. I have spoken of my career goals to my friends, who react with (hoomor). They think being an artist is a (nobel) profession, but wonder how I will make money. I (continu) to think of it as my dream job, though.

16. **career**
17. **suit**
18. **weary**
19. **easel**
20. **iris**
21. **soothing**
22. **bowl**
23. **humor**
24. **noble**
25. **continue**

SPELLING

Context Clues

You learned strategies for discovering word meanings in Unit 1. Looking at context clues, or information in the text around a word, can help you tackle an unknown word.

 **Read the following sentences from the selection "The Land I Lost: Adventures of a Boy in Vietnam." Pay close attention to the underlined words. Write your own definition for each underlined word, based on context clues.**

1. The family dog seemed to sense something was <u>amiss</u>, for he kept looking anxiously at everybody and whined from time to time. At midnight my mother went to my grandmother's room and found that she had died . . .

   amiss: **Answers will vary. The word means out of place; wrong**

2. One of her great passions was theater, and this passion never <u>diminished</u> with age. No matter how busy she was, she never missed a show when there was a group of actors in town.

   diminished: **Answers will vary. The word means became gradually less.**

3. I was born on the central highlands of Vietnam in a small <u>hamlet</u> . . . There were fifty houses in our <u>hamlet</u>, scattered along the river or propped against the mountainsides.

   hamlet: **Answers will vary. The word means a small village.**

4. I learned how to track game, how to recognize useful roots, how to distinguish <u>edible</u> mushrooms from poisonous ones.

   edible: **Answers will vary. The word means able to be eaten.**

▶ **Context Clues**

Practice

**Now that you have discovered the meanings of the
words *amiss*, *diminished*, *hamlet*, and *edible*, check
your definitions in the dictionary. Write your own
sentence containing each word.**

5. amiss: **Answers will vary.**

_____

_____

_____

6. diminished: **Answers will vary.**

_____

_____

_____

7. hamlet: **Answers will vary.**

_____

_____

_____

8. edible: **Answers will vary.**

_____

_____

_____

VOCABULARY

The /ow/ Sound

Word List

1. tower
2. however
3. pouch
4. towel
5. amount
6. powder
7. thousand
8. browse
9. pronounce
10. blouse
11. power
12. coward
13. account
14. pout
15. outward

Selection Words

16. downtown
17. mountains
18. surrounded
19. houses
20. hour

Pattern Study

The /ow/ sound is spelled *ow* at the ends of words, before a vowel, and before the letters *d*, *l*, *n*, and *s*. The /ow/ sound is also spelled *ou*.

▶ Write the spelling words with the /ow/ sound spelled *ow* before a vowel.

1. tower
2. however
3. towel
4. power
5. coward

▶ Write the spelling words with the /ow/ sound spelled *ow* before a consonant.

6. powder
7. browse
8. downtown

▶ Write the spelling words with the /ow/ sound spelled *ou*.

9. pouch
10. amount
11. thousand
12. pronounce
13. blouse
14. account
15. pout
16. outward
17. mountains
18. surrounded
19. houses
20. hour

UNIT 3 Heritage • **Lesson I** *The Land I Lost: Adventures of a Boy in Vietnam*

▶ **The /ow/ Sound**

Strategies

Visualization Strategy **The following spelling words are missing their /ow/ sounds. Write the words correctly in the spaces provided.**

21. t__er   **tower**

22. __tward   **outward**

23. th__sand   **thousand**

24. h__r   **hour**

25. p__er   **power**

26. am__nt   **amount**

27. p__t   **pout**

28. c__ard   **coward**

29. acc__nt   **account**

30. pron__nce   **pronounce**

31. p__ch   **pouch**

32. h__ses   **houses**

33. t__el   **towel**

34. br__se   **browse**

35. surr__nded   **surrounded**

SPELLING

UNIT 3 Heritage • **Lesson 2** *In Two Worlds: A Yup'ik Eskimo Family*

Concept Words

When you learn about a topic, you build your vocabulary by also learning certain words that help you understand and discuss that topic. These words are called concept words. For example, the selections "In Two Worlds: A Yup'ik Eskimo Family" and "History of the Tunrit" tell of the lifestyle of a different culture. To fully understand the stories, you must know the meanings of the concept words that specifically describe the Eskimo lifestyle, such as *tundra*, *harpooned*, *parka*, *kayak*, and *caribou*.

Below are groups of concept words that are used to write about a certain subject. Figure out the subject and write it on the line after each group. You may need to look some words up in the dictionary.

1. tulip, lily, iris, chrysanthemum   **flowers**

2. spatula, colander, grater, cleaver   **the kitchen**

3. steering wheel, radiator, battery, muffler   **car**

4. scissors, needle, thread, pattern   **sewing**

5. hard drive, monitor, floppy disk, mouse   **computers**

Concept Words

Practice

Choose a word from the following list of concept words describing Eskimo life that best completes each sentence. Look up the words in the dictionary to check your answers.

tundra	harpooned	parka	kayak	caribou

6. Alice wore a _____**parka**_____ to keep warm and dry in the snow.

7. The fishermen _____**harpooned**_____ a whale so they could use its oil.

8. We were snug in our _____**kayak**_____ as we paddled down the stream.

9. Many plants will not grow on the _____**tundra**_____, for it is a very cold and hard land.

10. The female _____**caribou**_____ is called a cow or a doe.

VOCABULARY

UNIT 3 Heritage • **Lesson 2** *In Two Worlds: A Yup'ik Eskimo Family*

The Final /əl/ Sound

Word List

1. title
2. final
3. level
4. middle
5. petal
6. sandal
7. model
8. dial
9. barrel
10. baffle
11. marvel
12. mammal
13. local
14. trial
15. signal

Selection Words

16. hospital
17. survival
18. metal
19. people
20. circle

Pattern Study

The final /əl/ sound is found in final unstressed syllables and can be spelled -*le*, -*el*, or -*al*.

▶ Write the spelling words with the final /əl/ sound spelled -*le*.

1. title
2. middle
3. baffle
4. people
5. circle

▶ Write the spelling words with the final /əl/ sound spelled -*el*.

6. level
7. model
8. barrel
9. marvel

▶ Write the spelling words with the final /əl/ sound spelled -*al*.

10. final
11. petal
12. sandal
13. dial
14. mammal
15. local
16. trial
17. signal
18. hospital
19. survival
20. metal

Name _____ Date _____

▶ **The Final /əl/ Sound**

Strategies

Family Strategy Write the spelling words on which the following words are based.

21. marvelous   **marvel** _____

22. locally   **local** _____

23. signaled   **signal** _____

24. dialing   **dial** _____

25. finally   **final** _____

Visualization Strategy Choose the correct spelling for the spelling words below. Write the correct word on the space provided.

26. circel, circle, circal   **circle** _____

27. title, tital, titel   **title** _____

28. hospitle, hospital, hospitel **hospital** _____

29. peopel, peopal, people   **people** _____

30. sandal, sandle, sandel   **sandal** _____

31. petel, petle, petal   **petal** _____

32. metal, metle, metel   **metal** _____

33. leval, level, levle   **level** _____

34. middel, middle, middal   **middle** _____

35. barrle, barral, barrel   **barrel** _____

SPELLING

UNIT 3 Heritage • **Lesson 3** *The West Side*

Spanish Words

As you read stories like the one told in the selection "The West Side," you may come across words from different languages, such as Spanish. These words help make the story more realistic by showing how the characters actually speak. You may not know the meanings of these words unless you speak that language yourself. But you can try to figure out the meaning from context clues.

Before you can discover the meanings of Spanish words, you must learn to recognize them in the texts you read. Spanish words frequently end with the vowels *a* or *o*. They may also have an *n* with a mark over it that looks like this: ñ. This mark is called a tilde.

 **Try It!** **Circle the five Spanish words in the paragraph below and write them in the spaces provided.**

My birthday party was full of fun and laughter. It was a real fiesta! When the other kids arrived, they brought colorful gifts and piled them on the table in the living room. Then the games began. We played Pin the Tail on the Donkey and Charades, and then we all tried to break the piñata, which was in the shape of a matador. When Eric finally broke it open with the broom handle, lots of candy and confetti came out all over us. After the games, we ate cake and ice cream, and had a fruit salad with papaya. I'm just glad we didn't have to eat my least favorite food—broccoli. Before I blew out my candles, Señor Brown led everyone as they sang "Happy Birthday." Then I opened my presents and thanked everyone very much as they left for home.

1. **fiesta**   3. **matador**   5. **Señor**

2. **piñata**   4. **papaya**

Name _____ Date _____

▶ Spanish Words

Practice

Here are the meanings in English for the Spanish words in the story on the previous page. After each meaning, write your own sentence containing each word.

6. *Fiesta* means "party" in English. ___Answers will___
   vary. _____

   _____

7. A *piñata* is a decorated container filled with candy or

   small toys that is broken open at a party. ___Answers___
   will vary. _____

   _____

8. A *matador* is a person who fights the bull in a bullfight.
   Answers will vary. _____

   _____

9. A *papaya* is an oblong, yellow fruit. ___Answers___
   will vary. _____

   _____

10. *Señor* is the same as the word *Mister* in English.
    Answers will vary. _____

    _____

VOCABULARY

UNIT 3   Heritage • **Lesson 3** *The West Side*

The /or/ and /är/ Sounds

Word List

1. pour
2. artist
3. parcel
4. adore
5. mortal
6. market
7. afford
8. starve
9. normal
10. barber
11. orbit
12. target
13. doorbell
14. force
15. warm

Selection Words

16. correct
17. garbage
18. cardboard
19. guitar
20. import

Pattern Study

The /or/ sound is usually spelled *or*, but can be spelled *ar*, *our*, *ore*, or *oor*. **The /är/ sound** is usually spelled *ar*.

▶ Write the spelling words with the /är/ sound spelled *ar*.

1. artist
2. parcel
3. market
4. starve
5. barber
6. target
7. garbage
8. cardboard
9. guitar

▶ Write the spelling words with the /or/ sound spelled *or*.

10. mortal
11. afford
12. normal
13. orbit
14. force
15. correct
16. import

▶ Write the spelling words with the /or/ sound spelled *our*, *ore*, and *oor*.

17. pour
18. adore
19. doorbell

▶ Write the spelling word with the /or/ sound spelled *ar*.

20. warm

► **The /or/ and /är/ Sounds**

SPELLING

Strategies

Dictionary Strategy Write the spelling words in alphabetical order.

21. adore
22. afford
23. artist
24. barber
25. cardboard
26. correct
27. doorbell
28. force
29. garbage
30. guitar
31. import
32. market
33. mortal
34. normal
35. orbit
36. parcel
37. pour
38. starve
39. target
40. warm

Meaning Strategy Write the spelling words that belong with each group.

41. weakness, hunger, empty   starve
42. scissors, towel, chair   barber
43. canvas, easel, watercolors   artist
44. strings, wood, music   guitar
45. food, shoppers, vendors   market
46. chime, visitor, entrance   doorbell

UNIT 3   Heritage • **Lesson 4** *Love as Strong as Ginger*

Levels of Specificity

You know that the word *specific* means "exact" or "precise." When writers want to describe something the best they can, they will try not to use a general word, but a word that is more specific and paints a certain picture for the reader. For example, the writer of "Love as Strong as Ginger" could have told us that the girl's grandmother taught her to make *food*, but instead stated that the grandmother taught her to make *dumplings*. The second word is more specific and gives us a clearer image of the story.

 **Try It!** These very general words are followed by more specific terms used in "Love as Strong as Ginger." Add another more specific word for the general term.

1. plant, bamboo,   **Answers will vary. Should be a kind of plant.**

2. fish, flounder,   **Answers will vary. Should be a kind of fish.**

3. herbs, chives,   **Answers will vary. Should be a kind of herb.**

4. tool, mallet,   **Answers will vary. Should be a kind of tool.**

5. vegetable, scallion,   **Answers will vary. Should be a vegetable.**

UNIT 3 Heritage • **Lesson 4** *Love as Strong as Ginger*

Levels of Specificity

Practice

In the following sentences, the underlined words are too general. Rewrite the sentences, replacing the underlined words with more specific words that mean the same thing. You will be surprised how much more interesting the sentences will be.

6. I decided to read that <u>book</u> because it was about <u>animals</u>.

Answers will vary.

_____

7. To get to the <u>building</u>, drive about five miles west on that <u>road</u>.

Answers will vary.

_____

8. We watched a <u>performance</u> at the theater, then went home in a <u>vehicle</u>.

Answers will vary.

_____

9. A <u>person</u> yelled at us when we swam out too far in the <u>water</u>.

Answers will vary.

_____

VOCABULARY

UNIT 3 Heritage • **Lesson 4** *Love as Strong as Ginger*

Consonant Blends

Word List

1. throat
2. stress
3. swallow
4. flavor
5. clothing
6. stubborn
7. profit
8. clinic
9. broken
10. blister
11. sparkle
12. startle
13. stumble
14. cruel
15. greedy

Selection Words

16. grandma
17. crowded
18. apron
19. sponges
20. starched

Pattern Study

Some common consonant blends are *cr, gr, thr, st, sw, fl, sp, br, bl,* and *cl.* Many consonant blends contain the letters *r* or *l.*

▶ Write the spelling words that begin with consonant blends with the letter *r.*

1. throat
2. stress
3. profit
4. broken
5. crowded
6. cruel
7. greedy
8. grandma
9. apron

▶ Write the spelling words that begin with consonant blends with the letter *l.*

10. flavor
11. clothing
12. clinic
13. blister

▶ Write the spelling words that begin with consonant blends containing *s,* but not *r.*

14. swallow
15. stubborn
16. sparkle
17. startle
18. stumble
19. sponges
20. starched

Consonant Blends • Spelling and Vocabulary Skills

UNIT 3 Heritage • **Lesson 4** *Love as Strong as Ginger*

Consonant Blends

Strategies

SPELLING

Pronunciation Strategy Write the spelling words that begin with the same consonant blends as the following words. Some words may have more than one answer.

21. clarify   clinic   clothing

22. thread   throat

23. bridge   broken

24. grand   greedy   grandma

25. strict   stress

26. blurry   blister

27. flight   flavor

Meaning Strategy Fill in the blanks with the spelling words that best complete each sentence.

28. That __starched__ shirt is so stiff it is uncomfortable.

29. Tie the __apron__ around your waist before you cook.

30. She is so __stubborn__ she won't even consider going skydiving.

31. It is __cruel__ to mistreat an animal.

32. What is your favorite __flavor__ of ice cream?

Antonyms

When you learned about the thesaurus in Unit 1, you worked with synonyms, or words that mean the same as other words. Antonyms are words that mean the opposite of other words. An antonym for *cold* is *hot*, and an antonym for *cheap* is *expensive.*

 **The words below are each followed by two other words. One is a synonym and one is an antonym for the first word. You will be asked to write either the synonym or the antonym in the spaces that follow.**

1. **continue**   extend   adjourn

   Which word is a synonym for *continue?*   **extend**

2. **mighty**   powerful   meek

   Which word is an antonym for *mighty?*   **meek**

3. **peculiar**   normal   odd

   Which word is an antonym for *peculiar?*   **normal**

4. **gleeful**   jovial   glum

   Which word is a synonym for *gleeful?*   **jovial**

5. **flexible**   unyielding   willing

   Which word is an antonym for *flexible?*   **unyielding**

UNIT 3 Heritage • **Lesson 5** *The Night Journey*

> **Antonyms**

Practice

The words below are from the selection "The Night Journey." They are followed by a synonym. Write an antonym for each word.

6. din

   synonym: noise

   antonym: _____ Answers will vary. _____

7. lambent

   synonym: glowing

   antonym: _____ Answers will vary. _____

8. inexorable

   synonym: unavoidable

   antonym: _____ Answers will vary. _____

9. ample

   synonym: plenty

   antonym: _____ Answers will vary. _____

10. obliterated

    synonym: destroyed

    antonym: _____ Answers will vary. _____

VOCABULARY

UNIT 3 Heritage • **Lesson 5** *The Night Journey*

Silent Letters

Word List

1. wristwatch
2. gnat
3. debt
4. autumn
5. folk
6. rhythm
7. known
8. sword
9. wrinkle
10. column
11. wrestle
12. doubt
13. gnaw
14. listen
15. yolk

Selection Words

16. whole
17. aisle
18. knob
19. rhymes
20. science

Pattern Study

Some common silent letters at the beginnings of words are *k* in *kn*, *g* in *gn*, and *w* in *wr*. Some common silent letters at the ends of words are *b* in *mb* and *n* in *mn*.

▶ Write the spelling words with a silent *w*.

1. wristwatch
2. sword
3. wrestle
4. wrinkle
5. whole

▶ Write the spelling words with a silent *h*.

6. rhythm
7. rhymes

▶ Write the spelling words with a silent *g*.

8. gnat
9. gnaw

▶ Write the spelling words with a silent *b* or a silent *l*.

10. debt
11. doubt
12. folk
13. yolk

▶ Write the spelling words with a silent *n*.

14. autumn
15. column

▶ Write the spelling words with a silent *k*.

16. known
17. knob

Silent Letters • Spelling and Vocabulary Skills

▶ **Silent Letters**

SPELLING

Strategies

Pronunciation Strategy **Write the silent consonant in the following words.**

18. science __c__

19. wristwatch __w__

20. sword __w__

21. column __n__

22. gnaw __g__

23. aisle __s__

24. whole __w__

25. rhymes __h__

26. folk __l__

27. doubt __b__

Visualization Strategy **The following spelling words are missing their silent letters. Write the words correctly.**

28. yok   **yolk**

29. nown   **known**

30. rinkle   **wrinkle**

31. autum   **autumn**

32. det   **debt**

33. lisen   **listen**

34. nat   **gnat**

35. rythm   **rhythm**

36. restle   **wrestle**

Review

Remember to keep using context clues to discover word meanings. You don't always have to go straight to the dictionary.

 **Try It!** The following sentences are from the selection "Parmele." Use context clues to figure out the meaning of the underlined word. Write a definition in the space provided.

1. Pa was a <u>sharecropper</u>. He worked in the fields, farming the land for the white man who owned it, and got paid in a share of the crops he raised.

   Definition: **Answers will vary. A sharecropper is a tenant farmer who works a person's land for an agreed share of the earnings from the crop.**

2. I remember her most bending over the <u>collards</u> in her garden or feeding the chickens.

   Definition: **Answers will vary. Collards are vegetables that can be grown in a garden.**

3. She used to sew leftover material from my dresses into her <u>patchwork</u> quilts.

   Definition: **Answers will vary. Patchwork is used to describe something made up of many different, mismatching parts.**

Name _____ Date _____

Practice

In the dictionary, check your definitions for the words on the previous page. Then write your own sentence containing each word.

4. sharecropper: Answers will vary.

_____

_____

_____

5. collards: Answers will vary.

_____

_____

_____

6. patchwork: Answers will vary.

_____

_____

_____

VOCABULARY

UNIT 3 Heritage • **Lesson 6** *Parmele*

Review

Word List

1. carpet
2. civil
3. countless
4. wrench
5. waffle
6. clover
7. shower
8. carve
9. glisten
10. steeple
11. gnarled
12. angle
13. crouch
14. cleats
15. popcorn

Selection Words

16. ankles
17. porches
18. stroke
19. thumb
20. around

Pattern Study

▶ Write the silent letter after each word.

1. wrench **w** _____   3. gnarled **g** _____

2. glisten **t** _____   4. thumb **b** _____

▶ Write the consonant blends in these words.

5. cleats **cl** _____   7. clover **cl** _____

6. steeple **st** _____   8. stroke **str** _____

▶ Write the letters that spell the /or/ and /är/ sounds in these words.

9. carve **ar** _____   11. popcorn **or** _____

10. carpet **ar** _____   12. porches **or** _____

▶ Write the letters that spell the final /əl/ sound in these words.

13. waffle **le** _____   15. civil **il** _____

14. angle **le** _____   16. ankles **le** _____

▶ Write the letters that spell the /ow/ sound in these words.

17. crouch **ou** _____   19. countless **ou** _____

18. shower **ow** _____   20. around **ou** _____

► **Review**

Strategies

Proofreading Strategy Circle the misspelled words in the paragraphs below and write them correctly in the spaces provided.

Dear Diary,

This morning, before I took my (shouer,) I took some time to watch the dew (glissen) in the sun. The mist was rising over the clover and the (narled) branches of the oak tree in the back yard. As I ate my waffle for breakfast, I reviewed for my history test on the (Civle) War.

At school, I poked my (thum) with my ruler as I was trying to draw a right angle. I forgot my (cleets) for gym class and nearly twisted both my (ankels) playing soccer. I did pass my history test, though!

After school, I had to ride (arond) the neighborhood on my bike and take care of my paper route. I took careful aim as I threw the papers on the porches. When the sun began to set behind the church (steepel) in the middle of town, I decided to head home for dinner. I wanted to have (popcoren,) but dad said we had to have pork chops and broccoli. Yuck!

21. shower
22. glisten
23. gnarled
24. Civil
25. thumb

26. cleats
27. ankles
28. around
29. steeple
30. popcorn

SPELLING

Social Studies Words

Try It! The following words can be found in the selection "... If You Lived at the Time of the American Revolution." They are social studies concept words that help tell of the American way of life in the 1770s and 1780s. Write the words next to their definitions. Try to figure out the definitions based on context clues or check them in a dictionary.

Loyalists	Patriots	neutral	Minutemen	inflation

1. People who, along with their families, no longer wanted the colonies to be under British rule.   **Patriots**

2. Men from Massachusetts who fought for independence in the Continental Army and could be ready to fight on "a minute's notice."   **Minutemen**

3. People who believed that the King of England had the right to rule the colonies.   **Loyalists**

4. A rise in the usual prices of goods and services.   **inflation**

5. Not taking sides or belonging to either side in a conflict.   **neutral**

Social Studies Words

Practice

Here are more social studies concept words from ". . . If You Lived at the Time of the American Revolution." See if you can place them correctly in the sentences.

| Stamp Act | Parliament | tyranny | Whigs | Quakers |

6. The **Stamp Act** of 1765 stated that colonists had to pay taxes on newspapers and land deeds.

7. The **Quakers** were pacifists, which meant they did not believe in fighting in the War.

8. The Patriots were also known as "Liberty Boys" and " **Whigs** ."

9. Some colonists resented the fact that the British **Parliament** was the governing body that made their rules.

10. The Patriots thought that the rule of the British was **tyranny** because they were taxed but were not represented in the British Parliament.

VOCABULARY

UNIT 4 Making a New Nation • **Lesson I** *...If You Lived at the Time of the American Revolution*

Plurals

Word List

1. zero
2. zeros
3. trio
4. trios
5. hero
6. heroes
7. echo
8. echoes
9. potato
10. potatoes
11. halo
12. halos
13. radios
14. buffalo
15. buffaloes

Selection Words

16. colonies
17. taxes
18. themselves
19. clothes
20. speeches

Pattern Study

To make many words plural, add *s* or *es*. For most words that end with a vowel and *o*, add *s* to make them plural. For most words that end with a consonant, then *o*, add *es* to make them plural. The letters *es* are also added to words ending with *ch*, *sh*, *s*, *ss*, *x*, *z*, or *zz*.

▶ Write the plural spelling words that end with a vowel and *o*, then *s*.

1. **trios**   2. **radios**

▶ Write the plural spelling words that end with a consonant and *o*, then *es*.

3. **heroes**   5. **potatoes**

4. **echoes**   6. **buffaloes**

▶ Write the plural spelling words that end with a consonant and *o*, then *s*.

7. **zeros**   8. **halos**

▶ Write the plural spelling words that end in a consonant, then *es*.

9. **taxes**   11. **speeches**

10. **clothes**   12. **themselves**

▶ Write the plural spelling word that ends in a vowel, then *es*.

13. **colonies**

UNIT 4 Making a New Nation • **Lesson I** *...If You Lived at the Time of the American Revolution*

Plurals

SPELLING

Strategies

Visualization Strategy Write the singular form of each spelling word.

14. speeches **speech**

15. taxes **tax**

16. halos **halo**

17. trios **trio**

18. potatoes **potato**

19. buffaloes **buffalo**

20. colonies **colony**

21. heroes **hero**

22. zeros **zero**

23. echoes **echo**

Meaning Strategy Write the spelling words that best complete the sentences.

24. Several _____**trios**_____ of singers, each consisting of a soprano, a tenor, and a bass, entertained the crowd.

25. The angel in the painting had a bright gold _____**halo**_____ around her head.

26. The soldiers who died in World War II were considered _____**heroes**_____.

27. Olivia had to give two _____**speeches**_____ at graduation because she was first in her class.

28. The students were proud of _____**themselves**_____ because they had all made discoveries in the science lab.

UNIT 4 Making a New Nation • **Lesson 2** *The Night the Revolution Began*

Synonyms

> You know that synonyms are words with the same, or nearly the same, meaning as other words. Remember that a word can have many synonyms that have slightly different meanings. You must use context clues to figure out which synonym is exactly right for a specific word in a sentence.

 **Choose the most appropriate synonym from the list to replace the underlined word in each sentence. Write the synonym you have chosen in the space that follows.**

1. The rip under your sleeve is not very <u>prominent</u>, but you should get it mended soon.

   pre-eminent   rugged   noticeable

   noticeable

2. Robert worked as an <u>apprentice</u> to a blacksmith so he could learn a trade.

   trainee   amateur   beginner

   trainee

3. The workers tried to <u>hoist</u> the barrels into the trucks.

   elevate   heighten   raise

   raise

4. The soldier hoped his superiors would not <u>discharge</u> him from the Army for his conduct.

   emit   dismiss   blast

   dismiss

5. We had a <u>rollicking</u> time at the square dance.

   sporty   jolly   romping

   jolly

▶ Synonyms

Practice

These words from "The Night the Revolution Began"
are followed by a synonym or an antonym. Write either
a synonym or an antonym for the word.

6. **disguising**
   antonym: unmasking

   synonym: **Answers will vary.**

7. **emerged**
   synonym: came out

   antonym: **Answers will vary.**

8. **objected**
   antonym: agreed

   synonym: **Answers will vary.**

9. **interfere**
   antonym: help

   synonym: **Answers will vary.**

10. **destroy**
    synonym: demolish

    antonym: **Answers will vary.**

VOCABULARY

UNIT 4 Making a New Nation • **Lesson 2** *The Night the Revolution Began*

Possessive Nouns

Word List

1. boys'
2. boss's
3. babies'
4. parents'
5. ladies'
6. girls'
7. pilot's
8. waiter's
9. director's
10. waitress's
11. officer's
12. owner's
13. teachers'
14. customer's
15. actor's

Selection Words

16. maker's
17. company's
18. ships'
19. king's
20. friend's

Pattern Study

To make a singular noun possessive, just add an apostrophe and *s*. Add an apostrophe and *s* even if the singular noun ends with an *s*. To make a plural noun possessive, just add an apostrophe at the end. If a plural noun does not end in an *s*, as is the case with *children*, add an apostrophe and *s*.

▶ Write the spelling words that are singular possessive nouns.

1. **boss's**
2. **pilot's**
3. **waitress's**
4. **officer's**
5. **customer's**
6. **friend's**
7. **company's**
8. **actor's**
9. **waiter's**
10. **director's**
11. **owner's**
12. **maker's**
13. **king's**

▶ Write the spelling words that are plural possessive nouns.

14. **boys'**
15. **babies'**
16. **parents'**
17. **ships'**
18. **girls'**
19. **ladies'**
20. **teachers'**

Possessive Nouns • Spelling and Vocabulary Skills

UNIT 4 Making a New Nation • **Lesson 2** *The Night the Revolution Began*

▶ **Possessive Nouns**

SPELLING

Strategies

Conventions Strategy Change these base words into singular or plural possessive nouns and write them on the lines below.

21. waitress (singular possessive)   **waitress's**

22. company (singular possessive)   **company's**

23. boss (singular possessive)   **boss's**

24. ship (plural possessive)   **ships'**

25. baby (plural possessive)   **babies'**

26. friend (singular possessive)   **friend's**

27. teacher (plural possessive)   **teachers'**

Proofreading Strategy Circle any words that are misspelled in the following sentences and write them correctly on the lines that follow. If all words in the sentence are spelled correctly, write the word *Correct* on the line.

28. The companie's employees will all get a bonus at the end of the year.   **company's**

29. Her boss'es desk is covered with papers and file folders.   **boss's**

30. The waitress's apron is covered with ketchup and grease.   **Correct**

31. Of all the babie's cries that could be heard in the nursery, hers was the loudest.   **babies'**

32. The girls' restroom needed more soap and paper towels.   **Correct**

Name _____ Date _____

Figurative Language

When a writer uses figurative language, he or she might use a metaphor, a simile, or personification.

A **metaphor** compares two unlike things by saying that one thing is another thing. For example, if you say *My brother's stomach is a bottomless pit*, you are comparing his stomach to a deep hole to describe how much he eats. You do not mean to say that his stomach actually *is* a bottomless pit. Metaphors are not meant to be taken literally.

A **simile** compares two things, as a metaphor does, but uses the words *like* or *as*. An example of a simile is *Your hands are as cold as ice*, or *Her eyes are like stars*.

Personification means giving human qualities to things that are not human, such as animals, plants, and objects. If you said that a star winked at you, you would be using personification.

 **Use the pairs of words below to write a sentence with a metaphor, a simile, and personification.**

1. Write a metaphor that uses the words *classroom* and *refrigerator*. **Answers will vary. Example: The freezing classroom is a refrigerator.**

2. Write a simile that uses the words *hard* and *diamonds*. **Answers will vary. Example: The candy was as hard as diamonds.**

3. Write a sentence using personification that contains the words *sun* and *smiled*. **Answers will vary. Example: The sun smiled on us all day.**

▶ **Figurative Language**

Practice

The following are examples of figurative language from "The Midnight Ride of Paul Revere." Notice how each simile, metaphor, and use of personification is worded and how clear a description each one makes. Then write the meaning of the underlined word. You can base your definition on context or look it up in a dictionary or thesaurus.

4. . . . just as the moon rose over the bay,
Where swinging wide at her <u>moorings</u> lay
The Somerset, British man-of-war . . .

Personification

Definition of *mooring:* A device that secures an object in place.

5. . . . A phantom ship, with each mast a <u>spar</u>
Across the moon like a prison bar . . .

Simile

Definition of *spar:* A strong wood or metal pole.

6. . . . That he could hear, like a <u>sentinel's</u> tread,
The watchful night-wind, as it went . . .

Simile

Definition of *sentinel:* Someone standing guard.

7. . . . He saw the <u>gilded</u> weathercock
Swim in the moonlight as he passed . . .

Metaphor

Definition of *gilded:* Having a covering of gold.

8. . . . And the meeting-house windows, blank and bare,
Gaze at him with a spectral glare,
As if they already stood <u>aghast</u> . . .

Personification

Definition of *aghast:* Feeling shocked or horrified.

VOCABULARY

UNIT 4 Making a New Nation • **Lesson 3** *The Midnight Ride of Paul Revere*

Compound Words

Word List

1. staircase
2. landmark
3. barefoot
4. campground
5. snowflake
6. earthquake
7. bookkeeper
8. typewriter
9. springtime
10. motorcycle
11. newspaper
12. granddaughter
13. sweatshirt
14. background
15. thunderstorm

Selection Words

16. meanwhile
17. moonlight
18. churchyard
19. landscape
20. overhead

Pattern Study

Compound words consist of two whole words that have been combined to form one word. These two words keep the same spellings when they are combined.

▶ The following spelling words are missing one of their base words. Write the whole compound words in the spaces provided.

1. news _____ **newspaper**

2. _____ cycle **motorcycle**

3. moon _____ **moonlight**

4. earth _____ **earthquake**

5. _____ shirt **sweatshirt**

6. _____ flake **snowflake**

7. grand _____ **granddaughter**

8. _____ ground **campground**

9. thunder _____ **thunderstorm**

10. _____ head **overhead**

11. bare _____ **barefoot**

12. back _____ **background**

13. _____ keeper **bookkeeper**

14. mean _____ **meanwhile**

Compound Words • Spelling and Vocabulary Skills

▶**Compound Words**

SPELLING

Strategies

Compound Word Strategy Write the spelling word that contains one of the base words in the following compound words.

15. campfire   **campground**

16. bookcase   **bookkeeper**

17. lighthouse   **moonlight**

18. headache   **overhead**

19. grandparent   **granddaughter**

Compound Word Strategy Write the spelling word formed by two of the words in each sentence.

20. She was a writer, but she could also type quickly.   **typewriter**

21. It's difficult to cycle up a hill without a motor.   **motorcycle**

22. The white flake on your coat is snow.   **snowflake**

23. A cemetery and a church are on the other side of our yard.   **churchyard**

24. My shirt was too heavy and I began to sweat.   **sweatshirt**

25. She purchased a grand piano for her daughter.   **granddaughter**

26. If you take off your sandal, your foot will be bare.   **barefoot**

27. We try to pitch our tents on dry ground when we camp.   **campground**

28. Fall is the time to plant bulbs that will come up in the spring.   **springtime**

Name _____ Date _____

Base Word Families

A base word can take many different forms when different prefixes, suffixes, and roots are added. The words in a base word family can be nouns, verbs, adjectives, or adverbs. When you know the meaning of the base word, you can begin to find the meanings of the words in the base word family.

 **Try It!** The following words are from the selection "The Declaration of Independence." They are followed by their base words. Write two more words with the same base word. Use the dictionary if you need help.

1. **hesitancy**

   Base word: hesitate

   Write two words with the base word *hesitate*.

   hesitated, hesitating, hesitant

2. **considerably**

   Base word: consider

   Write two words with the base word *consider*.

   considerate, reconsider, consideration

3. **endowed**

   Base word: endow

   Write two words with the base word *endow*.

   endowment, endowing

4. **philosophers**

   Base word: philosophy

   Write two words with the base word *philosophy*.

   philosophical, philosophic, philosophize

▶ **Base Word Families**

Practice

Now that you have thought of words in the same base word families, write two sentences for each family. One sentence will have the base word and the other sentence will have one of the related words you wrote.

5. hesitate: _Answers will vary._____

_____

word in the same family: _Answers will vary._____

_____

6. consider: _Answers will vary._____

_____

word in the same family: _Answers will vary._____

_____

7. endow: _Answers will vary._____

_____

word in the same family: _Answers will vary._____

_____

8. philosophy: _Answers will vary._____

_____

word in the same family: _Answers will vary._____

_____

VOCABULARY

UNIT 4 Making a New Nation • **Lesson 4** *The Declaration of Independence*

Changing y to i

Word List

1. heavy
2. heavier
3. worry
4. worried
5. envy
6. envious
7. butterfly
8. butterflies
9. daisy
10. daisies
11. bury
12. buried
13. supply
14. supplies
15. pastries

Selection Words

16. relied
17. earlier
18. copies
19. happiness
20. centuries

Pattern Study

When adding an ending like **-er, -ed, -ous,** or **-es** to a word ending in a consonant and a *y*, change the *y* to an *i*. If a word ends in a vowel and a *y*, just add the ending. Do not change the *y* to an *i* if the ending is **-ing.**

► Add the endings to the following base words and write the spelling words you have formed.

1. heavy + **-er** = **heavier**

2. daisy + **-es** = **daisies**

3. envy + **-ous** = **envious**

4. butterfly + **-es** = **butterflies**

5. supply + **-es** = **supplies**

6. pastry + **-es** = **pastries**

7. happy + **-ness** = **happiness**

8. early + **-er** = **earlier**

► Write the base words for each of these spelling words.

9. centuries **century**

10. copies **copy**

11. relied **rely**

12. worried **worry**

13. buried **bury**

UNIT 4 Making a New Nation • **Lesson 4** *The Declaration of Independence*

▶ Changing *y* to *i*

Strategies

Conventions Strategy Fill in the missing vowels in the following spelling words and write the complete words on the spaces provided.

14. heav__r   **heavier** _____

15. butterfl__s   **butterflies** _____

16. suppl__s   **supplies** _____

17. centur__s   **centuries** _____

18. env___s   **envious** _____

19. dais__s   **daisies** _____

20. pastr__s   **pastries** _____

Meaning Strategy Fill in the blank with the spelling word that best completes each sentence.

21. If you are _____**worried**_____ about being struck by lightning, seek shelter.

22. The school _____**supplies**_____ you need are pencils, erasers, scissors, and a ruler.

23. She got to school before me because she woke up _____**earlier**_____ .

24. Maya tried not to _____**envy**_____ her friend who had

   gotten a new bike for her birthday.

25. The _____**heavy**_____ backpack was difficult to carry and made her progress up the trail slow.

SPELLING

Words with Multiple Meanings

Many words have more than one meaning. You will often have to look at context clues to figure out which meaning is being used in a particular sentence.

 **Try It!** There are several meanings listed for the underlined word in each of these sentences. Put an *X* next to the meaning that is being used in the sentence.

1. She did not have enough <u>capital</u> to start her own business.

   a. Very good or satisfying; excellent. _____

   b. Money or property. __X___

   c. A large form of a letter of the alphabet. _____

2. Our dishwasher is <u>idle</u> because it is broken and needs a new part.

   a. Not wanting to be active; lazy. _____

   b. To run slowly and out of gear. _____

   c. Not working or being used. __X___

3. How long will it take to <u>shell</u> all those shrimp?

   a. To take something out of its shell. __X___

   b. To bombard with explosives. _____

   c. A hard outer covering. _____

UNIT 4 Making a New Nation • **Lesson 5** *The Master Spy of Yorktown*

▶ **Words with Multiple Meanings**

VOCABULARY

Practice

The underlined words in the following sentences have
several meanings. Write the meanings of the words as
they are used in the sentences.

4. Her family likes to <u>house</u> an exchange student every year.

house: **To give a place to live or stay**

5. It took a lot of <u>nerve</u> to swim across that river without a
life jacket.

nerve: **Courage or bravery**

6. We <u>embraced</u> the opportunity to become involved in our
community.

embraced: **Took up willingly**

7. They <u>surveyed</u> the damage left by the tornado and were
devastated.

surveyed: **Looked at or studied in detail**

8. Does your poor performance on the test still <u>trouble</u> you?

trouble: **To disturb or make uncomfortable**

9. Be careful that a piece of food does not get <u>lodged</u> in your
throat.

lodged: **Became stuck or fixed in one place**

10. I only saw him for an <u>instant</u>, and then he disappeared
into the crowd.

instant: **A moment**

Doubling Final Consonants

Word List

1. knotted
2. thinning
3. blurred
4. dropped
5. stirring
6. begged
7. starring
8. sobbed
9. fitting
10. dragged
11. fanned
12. petting
13. snapped
14. hopping
15. robbed

Selection Words

16. admitted
17. digging
18. trapping
19. hotter
20. winning

Pattern Study

If a word has one syllable and a short-vowel sound, and ends with one consonant, double the consonant before you add an ending, such as **-ing, -ed,** or **-er**. If a word has more than one syllable, double the final consonant if the last syllable is stressed. Do not double the final consonant if the last syllable is unstressed, or if the last syllable ends with two consonants or two vowels and a consonant.

▶ Add the endings to the following base words to write the spelling words.

1. win + **-ing** = **winning**
2. star + **-ing** = **starring**
3. sob + **-ed** = **sobbed**
4. drop + **-ed** = **dropped**
5. hop + **-ing** = **hopping**
6. thin + **-ing** = **thinning**
7. rob + **-ed** = **robbed**
8. beg + **-ed** = **begged**
9. snap + **-ed** = **snapped**
10. stir + **-ing** = **stirring**

UNIT 4 Making a New Nation • **Lesson 5** *The Master Spy of Yorktown*

▶ **Doubling Final Consonants**

SPELLING

Strategies

Family Strategy Write the spelling words that are related to the following words.

11. thinner   **thinning**

12. blurry   **blurred**

13. sobbing   **sobbed**

14. starred   **starring**

15. robbing   **robbed**

16. hopped   **hopping**

17. hottest   **hotter**

18. winner   **winning**

19. snapping   **snapped**

20. fitted   **fitting**

Meaning Strategy Fill in the blank with the spelling word that best completes each sentence.

21. The movers ____**dropped**____ the fragile vase and it shattered into many pieces.

22. My little brother enjoys ____**petting**____ the goats and sheep in the children's zoo.

23. Before air conditioning, people sat on their porches on a summer evening and ____**fanned**____ themselves.

24. I got tired of ____**stirring**____ the batter and decided to pour it in the pan.

25. Steven's shoelaces were ____**knotted**____ so tightly that he could not untie them.

UNIT 4 Making a New Nation • **Lesson 6** *Shh! We're Writing the Constitution*

Word Origins

If you see a Greek or Latin root you recognize in an otherwise unfamiliar word, you can begin to figure out the meaning of that word.

As you read the selection "Shh! We're Writing the Constitution," you will come across the word *revising*. You know that the prefix *re-* means "again," and you may know that the Latin root *vis*, which also appears in words like *vision* and *visual*, means "to see." So the word *revising* means "seeing again." When you revise something you have written, you look at it again and see what changes you should make.

 These words from "Shh! We're Writing the Constitution" contain some common Latin roots. Write another word that contains the same root.

1. judiciary

Write a word with the Latin root *jud*. **Answers will vary.**
Examples are judge, prejudge, judicial.

2. proceedings

Write a word with the Latin root *ceed*. **Answers will vary.**
Examples are succeed, proceed, exceed.

3. declaration

Write a word with the Latin root *clar*. **Answers will vary.**
Examples are declare, clarify, clarity.

UNIT 4 Making a New Nation • **Lesson 6** *Shh! We're Writing the Constitution*

▶ **Word Origins**

Practice

Now that you have thought of other words you know with the same Latin roots as the words from "Shh! We're Writing the Constitution," see if you can figure out their meanings. The meanings of the roots, prefixes, and suffixes are provided for you. Check your answers in a dictionary.

4. judiciary
jud = judge
ary = place for.

What does the noun *judiciary* mean? **A system of courts of law.**

5. proceedings
pro = forward
ceed = to go
ing = the continuing action of
s = plural

What does the noun *proceedings* mean? **Events that move forward.**

6. declaration
de = from
clar = clear
tion = state or quality of

What does the noun *declaration* mean? **An announcement or statement either spoken or written.**

VOCABULARY

Dropping *e* and Adding Endings

Word List

1. caring
2. writing
3. liking
4. smiling
5. staring
6. icing
7. owed
8. grading
9. chimed
10. shaky
11. behaved
12. escaping
13. polluted
14. puzzling
15. twinkling

Selection Words

16. united
17. described
18. revising
19. arrived
20. draped

Pattern Study

If a word ends in *e* and the ending begins with a vowel, drop the *e* before adding the ending.

▶ Add the endings to the following base words to write the spelling words.

1. care + *-ing* = **caring**
2. write + *-ing* = **writing**
3. like + *-ing* = **liking**
4. smile + *-ing* = **smiling**
5. stare + *-ing* = **staring**
6. ice + *-ing* = **icing**
7. owe + *-ed* = **owed**
8. grade + *-ing* = **grading**
9. chime + *-ed* = **chimed**
10. shake + *-y* = **shaky**
11. behave + *-ed* = **behaved**
12. escape + *-ing* = **escaping**
13. pollute + *-ed* = **polluted**
14. puzzle + *-ing* = **puzzling**
15. twinkle + *-ing* = **twinkling**

UNIT 4 Making a New Nation • **Lesson 6** *Shh! We're Writing the Constitution*

> **Dropping *e* and Adding Endings**

Strategies

Visualization Strategy **Fill in the missing vowels to write the spelling words.**

16. c_r_ng   caring
17. dr_p_d   draped
18. st_r_ng   staring
19. l_k_ng   liking
20. p_zzl_ng   puzzling

21. _sc_p_ng   escaping
22. wr_t_ng   writing
23. d_scr_b_d   described
24. p_ll_t_d   polluted
25. sm_l_ng   smiling

Family Strategy **Write the spelling words that are related to the following words.**

26. icy   icing
27. shaken   shaky
28. revision   revising
29. owing   owed
30. behavior   behaved
31. written   writing
32. arrival   arrived
33. graded   grading
34. twinkled   twinkling
35. chiming   chimed

SPELLING

UNIT·4 Making a New Nation • **Lesson 7** *We, the People of the United States*

►Review

The selections in this unit have all dealt with a specific time in American history. They have also contained many social studies words. These words will help you read and understand things about history, government, and people.

Try It!   The following social studies words can be found in the selection "We, the People of the United States." Write the words next to their definitions. Try to use context clues and check definitions in the dictionary only if you need to.

| tariffs | preamble | ratification | sects | despotism |

1. Religious groups **sects** _____

2. Charges or taxes that a government puts on goods coming into a country **tariffs** _____

3. Rule by a person with absolute power and authority
despotism _____

4. The introduction to a constitution **preamble** _____

5. The act of agreeing officially or approving **ratification** _____

Name _____ Date _____

Practice

Now that you know the definitions for these words, use each one in a sentence of your own. Make sure your sentence shows the meaning of the word.

6. tariffs: Answers will vary. _____

_____

_____

7. preamble: Answers will vary. _____

_____

_____

8. ratification: Answers will vary. _____

_____

_____

9. sects: Answers will vary. _____

_____

_____

10. despotism: Answers will vary. _____

_____

_____

VOCABULARY

UNIT 4   Making a New Nation • **Lesson 7** *We, the People of the United States*

Review

Word List

1. permitted
2. nighttime
3. striking
4. cousins'
5. blamed
6. inches
7. scoring
8. nineties
9. clipping
10. flurries
11. padded
12. trophies
13. scarecrow
14. indexes
15. skyscraper

Selection Words

16. presiding
17. derived
18. urging
19. astonishes
20. securing

Pattern Study

The spelling words provide examples of plural and possessive nouns, compound words, changing *y* to *i*, doubling final consonants, and dropping *e* to add endings.

▶ Write the spelling words that are related to the following base words. Notice how the base changes when an ending is added.

1. secure   **securing**
2. index   **indexes**
3. score   **scoring**
4. ninety   **nineties**
5. clip   **clipping**
6. urge   **urging**
7. pad   **padded**
8. permit   **permitted**
9. trophy   **trophies**
10. astonish   **astonishes**
11. blame   **blamed**
12. preside   **presiding**
13. cousins   **cousins'**

SPELLING

Strategies

Meaning Strategy Write the spelling word that goes with each group of concept words.

14. table of contents, appendix, pages   **indexes**

15. moon, stars, darkness   **nighttime**

16. measurement, ruler, feet   **inches**

17. building, steel, glass   **skyscraper**

18. straw, farmer, fields   **scarecrow**

Family Strategy Write the base words for the following spelling words.

19. permitted   **permit**

20. securing   **secure**

21. astonishes   **astonish**

22. striking   **strike**

23. clipping   **clip**

24. padded   **pad**

25. derived   **derive**

26. scoring   **score**

27. permitted   **permit**

28. urging   **urge**

Name _____ Date _____

Concept Words

As you learned in Unit 3, concept words are specific words used to write about and discuss a particular topic. When you talk about a new subject in your science or social studies class, read about a profession or hobby in a magazine, or even learn a new sport, you will come across new words that are related only to that topic. Make sure you understand the meanings of these new words so you can learn as much as you can about a new topic.

The selection "Sacagawea's Journey" contains a number of concept words related to boats and sailing. Read the following sentences, paying close attention to the underlined word. Write a definition for the word based on context clues. Check your answers in a dictionary.

1. The French traders covered all their beaver pelts and supplies in the shallow keelboat and used a long pole to propel it down the stream.

   What is a keelboat? **A keelboat is a shallow, covered boat used to carry supplies that is rowed, poled, or towed.**

2. Lewis and Clark and their Corps of Discovery traveled west on the Missouri River in several pirogues, or canoe-like boats.

   What is a pirogue? **A pirogue is a boat like a canoe.**

3. Charbonneau sat at the back of the boat and grasped the broad, flat moveable piece of wood called the rudder. This part allowed him to steer the boat through the rapids on the river.

   What is a rudder? **A rudder is a broad, flat, movable piece of wood or metal attached to the rear of a boat and used in steering.**

UNIT 5 Going West • **Lesson I** *Sacagawea's Journey*

Practice

Here are some more concept words from "Sacagawea's Journey" that are related to the topic of sailing. Read the definitions and write your own sentence containing each word.

4. tributary: A river or stream that flows into a larger river.

Answers will vary.
_____

_____

5. portage: The act of carrying boats over land when water passage is dangerous or impossible.

Answers will vary.
_____

_____

6. mast: A tall pole on a sailing ship or boat that supports the sails.

Answers will vary.
_____

_____

7. shoals: Places in a river, lake, or ocean where the water is shallow.

Answers will vary.
_____

_____

VOCABULARY

UNIT 5 Going West • **Lesson 1** *Sacagawea's Journey*

Homophones

Pattern Study

Homophones are words that sound the same but have different spellings and meanings.

Word List

1. tied
2. tide
3. stake
4. steak
5. hymn
6. horse
7. hoarse
8. throne
9. thrown
10. sweet
11. suite
12. brake
13. break
14. reel
15. real

Selection Words

16. plain
17. plane
18. waist
19. waste
20. heard

▶ Write the spelling word that is a homophone for each of the following words.

1. tied   **tide**
2. steak   **stake**
3. him   **hymn**
4. throne   **thrown**
5. sweet   **suite**
6. horse   **hoarse**
7. brake   **break**
8. real   **reel**
9. plane   **plain**
10. waste   **waist**
11. herd   **heard**
12. thrown   **throne**
13. tide   **tied**
14. plain   **plane**
15. hoarse   **horse**

UNIT 5 Going West • **Lesson I** *Sacagawea's Journey*

▶ Homophones

SPELLING

Strategies

Meaning Strategy **Fill in each blank with the spelling word that best completes the sentence. Be sure to choose the correct homophone for the meaning of each sentence.**

16. The corsets of the nineteenth century made a woman's _____**waist**_____ as small as 18 inches around.

17. The fans were _____**hoarse**_____ from shouting and screaming at the soccer game.

18. Our hotel _____**suite**_____ had a living area and a small kitchen.

19. The man _____**heard**_____ a dog barking in the night.

20. When the _____**tide**_____ is high on the beach, the sand castles will be washed away.

Meaning Strategy **Write the correct spelling word next to each definition.**

21. without decoration _____**plain**_____

22. actual or true; not imagined _____**real**_____

23. a stick or post pointed at one end _____**stake**_____

24. to use or spend in a careless or useless way _____**waste**_____

25. a group of connected rooms _____**suite**_____

UNIT 5   Going West • **Lesson 2** *Buffalo Hunt*

Synonyms

Remember that synonyms are words with similar meanings. A word can have many synonyms with slightly different meanings. When choosing a synonym, make sure it fits in with the words around it and makes sense in the context.

 **Try It!**   The following words are from the selection "Buffalo Hunt." Find two synonyms for each vocabulary word in the word list and write them next to the word. Look in a dictionary or thesaurus if you do not know the meanings of the vocabulary words.

1. procession   **parade**   **a march**
2. gorged   **ate**   **devoured**
3. seared   **charred**   **burned**
4. dwindle   **decrease**   **diminish**
5. sufficient   **enough**   **adequate**

expert	devoured	decrease	diminish
charred	a march	build	adequate
skilled	job	parade	lacking
ate	scooped	fixed	cheat
enough	burned	starved	secured

UNIT 5 Going West • **Lesson 2** *Buffalo Hunt*

Synonyms

Practice

Put an *X* next to the synonym that best replaces the underlined word in each of these sentences from "Buffalo Hunt." Use context clues to choose a word that has exactly the right meaning.

6. As Indian girls grew up, they learned from their mothers and grandmothers the art of transforming a dead buffalo into a thousand practical and useful objects.

articles __X__   opposes _____   wishes _____

7. Under the right conditions, the Indians could get better results with less danger by hunting in the old way—on foot.

restrictions _____   ailments _____   circumstances __X__

8. And as railroads were built across the prairies and plains, white hunters furnished buffalo meat for the railroad construction crews.

armed _____   decorated _____   supplied __X__

9. Organized bands of hide hunters shot their way south from Kansas to Texas.

ribbons _____   groups __X__   ensembles _____

10. On the Great Plains of North America, every Indian tribe had a rich and ready store of buffalo tales and legends.

stock __X__   shop _____   market _____

VOCABULARY

UNIT 5 Going West • **Lesson 2** *Buffalo Hunt*

Words with *dis-* and *mis-*

Word List

1. mistook
2. dislike
3. disagree
4. mistreat
5. disloyal
6. discover
7. misspell
8. disgrace
9. mislaid
10. misprint
11. displease
12. disconnect
13. mislead
14. misjudge
15. distrust

Selection Words

16. distance
17. distinct
18. disappear
19. disturb
20. discuss

Pattern Study

Many words feature the prefixes **mis-** and **dis-**. The prefix **dis-** means "not" or "apart." The prefix **mis-** means "bad." The spelling of the base word does not change when **mis-** or **dis-** is added.

▶ Add the prefix **mis-** or **dis-** to each of these base words to write the spelling words.

1. like   **dislike**
2. took   **mistook**
3. trust   **distrust**
4. grace   **disgrace**
5. judge   **misjudge**
6. lead   **mislead**
7. connect   **disconnect**
8. treat   **mistreat**
9. print   **misprint**
10. cover   **discover**
11. appear   **disappear**
12. spell   **misspell**
13. loyal   **disloyal**
14. laid   **mislaid**
15. please   **displease**

Name _____ Date _____

UNIT 5 Going West • **Lesson 2** *Buffalo Hunt*

Words with *dis-* and *mis-*

SPELLING

Strategies

Visualization Strategy Fill in the missing letters and write the whole spelling words.

16. __ i __ cuss **discuss**
17. __ i __ cover **discover**
18. __ i __ laid **mislaid**
19. __ i __ trust **distrust**
20. __ i __ lead **mislead**
21. __ i __ like **dislike**
22. __ i __ appear **disappear**
23. __ i __ judge **misjudge**
24. __ i __ agree **disagree**
25. __ i __ tinct **distinct**

Family Strategy Write the spelling word that is related to each of the following words.

26. mistaken **mistook**
27. connection **disconnect**
28. discussion **discuss**
29. spelling **misspell**
30. agreement **disagree**

Words with Multiple Meanings

As you read, you will come across many words that have more than one meaning. You will also notice that in the dictionary there are a number of entries with more than one definition. Words with multiple meanings can be confusing, but you can discover which meaning is being used by looking at context clues.

The following words from "The Journal of Wong Ming-Chung: A Chinese Miner" have multiple meanings. One definition is provided for you. Use context clues or the dictionary to write a different definition for each word.

1. rockers: Rocking chairs.

   Another definition of *rockers* is _**Answers will vary.**_____

2. prospect: Something looked forward to or expected.

   Another definition of *prospect* is _**Answers will vary.**_____

3. lumber: To move about in a clumsy, noisy way.

   Another definition of *lumber* is _**Answers will vary.**_____

4. registered: Showed or expressed.

   Another definition of *registered* is _**Answers will vary.**_____

5. deposits: Large amounts of a mineral in rock or in the ground.

   Another definition of *deposits* is _**Answers will vary.**_____

Name _____   Date _____

UNIT 5 Going West • **Lesson 3** *The Journal of Wong Ming-Chung:*
A Chinese Miner

▶ Words with Multiple Meanings

Practice

Below are the vocabulary words from the previous page, along with a definition for each word. Use each word in one sentence of your own. Make sure the meaning given fits the word in your sentence.

6. rockers: Rocking chairs.

7. prospect: To search or explore, as for gold.

8. lumber: To move about in a clumsy, noisy way.

9. registered: Had one's name placed on a list or record.

10. deposits: Puts something in a bank account.

VOCABULARY

Spelling and Vocabulary Skills • *Multiple Meanings*   UNIT 5 • Lesson 3   **115**

Words with -ent and -ant

Word List

1. agent
2. tolerant
3. resident
4. present
5. assistant
6. different
7. permanent
8. prominent
9. apparent
10. dependent
11. confident
12. represent
13. violent
14. recent
15. continent

Selection Words

16. immigrant
17. important
18. protectant
19. insistent
20. hesitant

Pattern Study

Many words feature the suffixes **-ent** and **-ant**. These suffixes mean "one who performs" when added to words to make them nouns. The suffixes mean "inclined to," "performing," or "being" when added to words to make them adjectives.

▶ Add the suffix **-ent** or **-ant** to the following word bases and write the spelling words.

1. ag____   **agent**

2. toler____   **tolerant**

3. resid____   **resident**

4. pres____   **present**

5. assist____   **assistant**

6. differ____   **different**

7. perman____   **permanent**

8. promin____   **prominent**

9. appar____   **apparent**

10. depend____   **dependent**

11. confid____   **confident**

Words with -ent and -ant

Strategies

Proofreading Strategy Circle the misspelled words in the following sentences and write them correctly in the spaces provided.

12. When we adopted Sparky from the Humane Society, he became a (permenant) member of our family.

permanent

13. At first, Mom and Dad were afraid Sparky would not be (tolerent) of the baby pulling on his fur. **tolerant**

14. The black ring around Sparky's left eye is a (prominant) feature. **prominent**

15. Sometimes late at night, Sparky will run to the fence and bark furiously for no (apparant) reason. **apparent**

Visualization Strategy Circle the words that are spelled correctly and write them on the lines that follow.

16. tolerent (tolerant) **tolerant**

17. permanant (permanent) **permanent**

18. (dependent) dependint **dependent**

19. apparant (apparent) **apparent**

20. (confident) confedant **confident**

SPELLING

Name _____ Date _____

Foreign Words

> As you read, you will come across words that may be unfamiliar to you because they come from different languages than English. As people speak and write in English, they sometimes use words from Spanish, French, German, Italian, Japanese, or even African languages like Swahili to make their ideas more specific and interesting.
>
> **French words: crochet, amateur, ballet, beret, mirage**
> **Spanish words: marina, bolero, pronto, patio**
> **Italian words: ballerina, macaroni, gusto, mascara**

The following words are Spanish words from the selection "The Coming of the Long Knives." Fill in the blank in each of the sentences with the word that fits best. You will use each word once.

Navaho	mesa	piñon trees	pinto beans	canyon

1. Her ancestors were Native Americans and members of the
   _____ **Navaho** _____ tribe of northern New Mexico.

2. The recipe calls for tortillas, tomatoes, green chilies, and
   pinto beans _____.

3. The red rocks rose on either side of us as we drifted down the
   stream that cut through the _____ **canyon** _____.

4. The shade of the _____ **piñon trees** _____ was not enough to keep us
   cool on that blistering summer day.

5. We stood on the flat top of the _____ **mesa** _____ and looked out
   across the barren land of the desert.

▶ **Foreign Words**

Practice

Now that you have an idea of what each of the Spanish words from "The Coming of the Long Knives" means, use each word in a sentence of your own.

6. pinto beans: Answers will vary.

_____

_____

7. Navaho: Answers will vary.

_____

_____

8. mesa: Answers will vary.

_____

_____

9. canyon: Answers will vary.

_____

_____

10. piñon trees: Answers will vary.

_____

_____

VOCABULARY

UNIT 5 Going West • **Lesson 4** *The Coming of the Long Knives*

Words with *-tion, -sion,* or *-sure*

Word List

1. explosion
2. vision
3. examination
4. measure
5. position
6. discussion
7. edition
8. pleasure
9. version
10. education
11. tradition
12. selection
13. collision
14. restriction
15. illusion

Selection Words

16. nation
17. direction
18. destruction
19. starvation
20. duration

Pattern Study

Nouns are formed when the endings *-tion,* *-sion,* and *-sure* are added to words. The ending *-tion* occurs more often than *-sion.* The ending *-sion* is often used to form a noun from a verb ending with *-ss* or *-mit.*

▶ Write the spelling words that end with *-tion.*

1. examination
2. edition
3. tradition
4. restriction
5. direction
6. starvation
7. position
8. education
9. selection
10. nation
11. destruction
12. duration

▶ Write the spelling words that end with *-sion.*

13. explosion
14. discussion
15. collision
16. vision
17. version
18. illusion

▶ Write the spelling words that end with *-sure.*

19. measure
20. pleasure

▶ Words with *-tion*, *-sion*, or *-sure*

Strategies

Visualization Strategy Fill in the missing letters and write the spelling words correctly on the lines below.

21. posi___n   **position** _____

22. edi___n   **edition** _____

23. tradi___n   **tradition** _____

24. na___n   **nation** _____

25. direc___n   **direction** _____

26. destruc___n   **destruction** _____

27. illu___n   **illusion** _____

28. mea___e   **measure** _____

29. dura___n   **duration** _____

30. ver___n   **version** _____

Family Strategy Write the spelling word that is related to each of the following words.

31. educated   **education** _____

32. collide   **collision** _____

33. exploding   **explosion** _____

34. discussed   **discussion** _____

35. restricted   **restriction** _____

SPELLING

Name _____ Date _____

Similes

> Similes are comparisons between two things using the word *like* or *as.* Examples of similes include:
>
> ▸ **She was as gentle as a lamb.**
> ▸ **Her brain was like a sponge.**
> ▸ **He is as strong as a lion.**

 **The following sentences from "Old Yeller and the Bear" contain similes. See if you can locate the similes. Then write what two things are being compared in each simile.**

1. One time he brought in a horned toad that got so mad he swelled out round and flat as a Mexican tortilla . . . And once he turned out of his pocket a wadded-up baby copperhead that nearly threw Mama into spasms.

   The simile compares ____**a toad**____ to ____**a tortilla**____.

2. A minute before, I'd been so tired out with my rail splitting that I couldn't have struck a trot. But now I raced through the tall trees in that creek bottom, covering ground like a scared wolf.

   The simile compares ____**the boy, or I**____ to ____**a wolf**____.

3. It was that big yeller dog. He was roaring like a mad bull.

   The simile compares ____**the dog**____ to ____**a bull**____.

4. I saw the bear lunge up to stand on her hind feet like a man while she clawed at the body of the yeller dog hanging to her throat.

   The simile compares ____**the bear**____ to ____**a man**____.

5. I . . . slung him toward Mama like he was a half-empty sack of corn.

   The simile compares ____**the boy, or him**____ to ____**a sack of corn**____.

▶ **Similes**

Practice

Place an *X* in the blank next to each sentence that has a simile.

6. The newborn baby is as light as a feather. __X__

7. That used car is nothing but a lemon. _____

8. I was so exhausted I slept like a log. __X__

9. After he sat on the straw hat, it was as flat as a pancake.
   __X__

10. I like him because he has a heart of gold. _____

11. The gentle breeze playfully tapped me on the cheek.

    _____

12. The lake was so calm that it was as smooth as glass.
    __X__

13. He was being a chicken when he wouldn't go to the

    dentist. _____

14. The superhero in that comic book is a streak of lightning

    when he flies through the air. _____

15. She eats like a bird at lunch, and then is starving at

    dinnertime. __X__

VOCABULARY

UNIT 5 Going West • **Lesson 5** *Old Yeller and the Bear*

Words with -ed and -ing

Word List

1. whispering
2. pulled
3. propped
4. shopping
5. wagged
6. planned
7. waited
8. handling
9. followed
10. gardening
11. paying
12. stepping
13. crawling
14. tracing
15. weeding

Selection Words

16. captured
17. catching
18. ached
19. poured
20. scrambling

Pattern Study

If a word ends in *e*, drop the *e* before adding the endings **-ed** and **-ing**. If a word ends with a short vowel followed by a single consonant, double the consonant before adding the endings **-ed** and **-ing**.

▶ Write the spelling words that drop the final *e* before adding **-ed** or **-ing**.

1. captured
2. handling
3. scrambling
4. ached
5. tracing

▶ Write the spelling words that double the final consonants before adding **-ed** or **-ing**.

6. propped
7. planned
8. stepping
9. wagged
10. shopping

▶ Write the spelling words whose base words were not changed to add **-ed** or **-ing**.

11. pulled
12. waited
13. whispering
14. paying
15. weeding
16. poured
17. followed
18. gardening
19. crawling
20. catching

UNIT 5 Going West • **Lesson 5** *Old Yeller and the Bear*

▶ **Words with -ed and -ing**

Strategies

Family Strategy Write the spelling word that is related to each of the following words.

21. prop   **propped**

22. wait   **waited**

23. handle   **handling**

24. trace   **tracing**

25. ache   **ached**

26. scramble **scrambling**

27. shop   **shopping**

28. plan   **planned**

29. follow   **followed**

30. crawl   **crawling**

31. pour   **poured**

32. step   **stepping**

33. weed   **weeding**

34. whisper **whispering**

35. wag   **wagged**

SPELLING

Compound Words

Compound words are created by combining two words. Often, you can figure out the definition of a compound word by breaking it into two words and defining each one. Then think of how the two definitions could be related in one word.

For example, the compound word **downpour** is formed from the words **down** and **pour. Down** is the opposite of **up** and **pour** is related to the flowing of liquids. When we put these definitions together, we see that a downpour is a flowing down of a liquid, in this case rain.

 **Try It!** **Each of the following sentences contains two underlined words that can be combined to form a compound word from "Bill Pickett: Rodeo-Ridin' Cowboy." Write the compound word after each sentence.**

1. When we got <u>home</u>, we found that grandma had <u>spun</u> all the wool into thread. **homespun** _____

2. When he discovered he was late, he jumped out of <u>bed</u> and got into his <u>clothes</u>. **bedclothes** _____

3. That <u>blue</u> dress looks pretty with a <u>bonnet</u>. **bluebonnet** _____

4. At the end of the day, the <u>stock</u> were herded into the <u>yards</u>. **stockyards** _____

5. If I'm going to milk this <u>cow</u>, I'll need a <u>hand</u>. **cowhand** _____

▶ **Compound Words**

VOCABULARY

Practice

The vocabulary words on the previous page from "Bill Pickett: Rodeo-Ridin' Cowboy" are broken down into their parts below. Write a definition for each part. Then write a definition for the whole word based on your other definitions.

6. home: A place where a person lives.

spun: Made thin fiber into thread.

homespun: A word used to describe a cloth woven by hand at home, not in a factory.

7. bed: Something used to sleep or rest on.

clothes: Things worn to cover the body.

bedclothes: The coverings, like sheets or blankets, used on a bed.

8. stock: Cattle, sheep, and other animals raised on a farm or ranch.

yards: Enclosed areas of ground.

stockyards: Enclosed places with pens and sheds where farm or ranch animals are kept.

9. cow: An animal that produces milk.

hand: A person who works; a laborer.

cowhand: A person who works on a cattle ranch or farm.

UNIT 5 Going West • **Lesson 6** *Bill Pickett: Rodeo-Ridin' Cowboy*

Words with -er and -est

Word List

1. happiest
2. wiser
3. slimmer
4. calmest
5. dishonest
6. container
7. scariest
8. daughter
9. easiest
10. saltier
11. cheaper
12. dirtiest
13. farthest
14. nearest
15. loser

Selection Words

16. loudest
17. feistiest
18. closer
19. greater
20. harshest

Pattern Study

If a word ends in *e*, drop the *e* before adding *-er* or *-est*. If a word ends with a short vowel and a consonant, double the consonant before adding *-er* or *-est*. If a word ends in *y*, change the *y* to *i* before adding *-er* or *-est*.

▶ Add the ending *-er* or *-est* to the following word bases and write the spelling words. Double the final consonant or change the *y* to *i* when necessary before adding the ending.

1. happy + *-est* = **happiest**
2. salty + *-er* = **saltier**
3. contain + *-er* = **container**
4. near + *-est* = **nearest**
5. feisty + *-est* = **feistiest**
6. wise + *-er* = **wiser**
7. scary + *-est* = **scariest**
8. dirty + *-est* = **dirtiest**
9. slim + *-er* = **slimmer**
10. harsh + *-est* = **harshest**

UNIT 5 Going West • **Lesson 6** *Bill Pickett: Rodeo-Ridin' Cowboy*

Words with -er and -est

SPELLING

Strategies

Meaning Strategy Fill in the blanks with spelling words that make the most sense in each sentence.

11. The experienced actor was the ____calmest____ one at the show; he didn't have sweaty palms and a racing heart like the amateurs.

12. After months of exercising and eating healthful foods, he was much ____slimmer____.

13. The motorcycle racer who wrecked in the mud was the ____dirtiest____ contestant at the end of the race.

14. After the temperature dipped below zero for the tenth day in a row, we decided it had been the ____harshest____ winter ever.

15. I decided it would be ____wiser____ to go to bed early so I could get plenty of sleep before my test.

Visualization Strategy Fill in the missing vowels and write the spelling words on the lines below.

16. gr__t_r ____greater____

17. __s__st ____easiest____

18. c_nt__n_r ____container____

19. l_s_r ____loser____

20. d_sh_n_st ____dishonest____

Review

When you take the time to discover the meanings of concept words, and find synonyms and multiple meanings for a word, you are helping your vocabulary grow.

 **Write a definition for the underlined word based on context clues. You may use a dictionary if you need help.**

The bloodsucking <u>rapscallions</u> could be mighty pesky, but we'd learn to distract them.

1. What is a *rapscallion?* **Answers will vary. A rapscallion is a rascal.**

Many a time, before dawn, a rapping at the windows would wake us out of a sound sleep. It was those <u>confounded</u>, needlenosed gallinippers pecking away, demanding breakfast.

2. What does *confounded* mean in this sentence? **Answers will vary. Confounded means dreadful or hateful.**

The earth was so <u>parched</u>, we couldn't raise a crop of beets and the varmints were getting downright <u>ornery</u> . . . "Thunderbolt!" I exclaimed, "our topsoil's so dry it's gone in reverse."

3. What does *parched* mean? **Answers will vary. Parched means extremely dry.**

4. What does *ornery* mean? **Answers will vary. Ornery means having a cranky disposition.**

Practice

These words from "McBroom the Rainmaker" are followed by synonyms and antonyms. Write an *s* next to the synonyms and an *a* next to the antonyms.

5. rapscallions

mischief-makers   **s** _____

saints   **a** _____

rascals   **s** _____

6. parched

dried   **s** _____

moistened   **a** _____

juicy   **a** _____

7. confounded

hateful   **s** _____

delightful   **a** _____

dreadful   **s** _____

8. ornery

angelic   **a** _____

well-behaved   **a** _____

mean-spirited   **s** _____

VOCABULARY

Review

Word List

1. pedal
2. vain
3. promotion
4. laziest
5. evident
6. misfire
7. mission
8. peddle
9. disprove
10. carrying
11. vein
12. traction
13. mismatch
14. decent
15. branched

Selection Words

16. disposition
17. harvested
18. smallest
19. shrinking
20. dried

Pattern Study

The spelling words are examples of homophones, words with **dis-** and **mis-**, words with **-ent**, words with **-tion** and **-sion**, words with **-ed** and **-ing**, and words with **-est**.

▶ Write the spelling words that are homophones.
1. pedal
2. peddle
3. vein
4. vain

▶ Write the spelling words with **dis-** and **mis-**.
5. misfire
6. disprove
7. mismatch

▶ Write the spelling words with **-ent**.
8. decent
9. evident

▶ Write the spelling words with **-tion** and **-sion**.
10. traction
11. mission
12. promotion
13. disposition

▶ Write the spelling words with the endings **-ed** and **-ing**.
14. carrying
15. branched
16. dried
17. shrinking
18. harvested

UNIT 5 Going West • **Lesson 7** *McBroom the Rainmaker*

▶Review

Strategies

Family Strategy Write the spelling word that is related to each word below.

19. promoted   **promotion**

20. evidence   **evident**

21. dry   **dried**

22. improve   **disprove**

23. fiery   **misfire**

24. unmatched   **mismatch**

25. peddler   **peddle**

26. vanity   **vain**

27. harvesting   **harvested**

28. lazy   **laziest**

29. decency   **decent**

30. branching   **branched**

31. carried   **carrying**

32. pedaling   **pedal**

SPELLING

Personification

When you learned about figurative language, you discovered that when a writer uses personification, he or she gives a human quality to something that is not human. Here is an example of personification:

The snowflakes dipped and twirled and danced together in circles as they jumped from the clouds above.

 **Try It!** After each sentence, write what is being personified. Then write a definition for the underlined word based on context clues.

1. The little boat was filled with a terrible sense of danger as

   it began its <u>perilous</u> journey through the rapids. _____**boat**_____

   perilous: _____**dangerous**_____

2. The workers tried to move it, but the rock was stubborn

   and determined not to be <u>swayed</u>. _____**rock**_____

   swayed: _____**moved**_____

3. The stars were in awe, and thought the moon a <u>wondrous</u>

   sight. _____**stars**_____

   wondrous: _____**to be marveled at**_____

4. The bridge was proud of its mighty presence as it <u>spanned</u>

   the great river. _____**bridge**_____

   spanned: **stretched across**

UNIT 6 Journeys and Quests • **Lesson I** *The Story of Jumping Mouse*

 **Personification**

Practice

Use the object and the action given to write your own sentences containing personification. Be creative and paint a detailed picture with your sentence. Example: *The little mouse wrote a pitiful letter to the cat, begging him to stop his constant stalking.*

5. mouse   wrote: **Answers will vary.**

_____

_____

6. clarinet   sang: **Answers will vary.**

_____

_____

7. wind   screamed: **Answers will vary.**

_____

_____

8. horse   laughed: **Answers will vary.**

_____

_____

VOCABULARY

UNIT 6 Journeys and Quests • **Lesson I** *The Story of Jumping Mouse*

Greek Roots

Word List

1. telephone
2. microphone
3. microchip
4. microscope
5. photograph
6. phonograph
7. photo
8. graph
9. centimeter
10. kilometer
11. television
12. millimeter
13. telegraph
14. geography
15. alphabet
16. automobile
17. astronaut
18. unicycle
19. biography
20. biology

Pattern Study

Understanding the meanings of Greek roots can help you spell many new words. Here are some of the Greek roots in the spelling words and their meanings.

micro = small   *tele* = far off
graph = to write   *bio* = life
geo = earth   *astr* = star
ology = study of   *phon* = sounds
photo = light   *cycl* = circle
meter = measure   *auto* = self

▶ Fill in the Greek root and write the whole spelling word.

1. centi _____ **centimeter** _____

2. _____ mobile **automobile** _____

3. milli _____ **millimeter** _____

4. _____ chip **microchip** _____

5. _____ bet **alphabet** _____

6. _____ vision **television** _____

7. _____ logy **biology** _____

8. phono _____ **phonograph** _____

9. _____ phone **telephone** _____

10. uni _____ **unicycle** _____

UNIT 6 Journeys and Quests • **Lesson I** *The Story of Jumping Mouse*

▶**Greek Roots**

Strategies

Meaning Strategy Write the spelling word that is represented by the following Greek root meaning combinations.

11. life + study of = **biology**

12. small + sounds = **microphone**

13. earth + to write = **geography**

14. light + to write = **photograph**

15. far off + sounds = **telephone**

Family Strategy Write a spelling word that contains the same Greek root as each of the following words. Some words will have more than one correct answer.

16. astronomy **astronaut**

17. bicycle **unicycle**

18. automatic **automobile**

19. biosphere **biography or biology**

20. odometer **centimeter, kilometer, or millimeter**

21. microwave **microphone, microchip, or microscope**

22. geothermal **geography**

23. televise **telephone, television, or telegraph**

24. psychology **biology**

25. graphite **photograph, phonograph, graph, telegraph, or biography**

SPELLING

UNIT 6 Journeys and Quests • **Lesson 2** *Trapped by the Ice!*

Homophones

Homophones are words that sound the same but have different spellings and meanings. The following word pairs are examples of homophones.

ball	bare	fair	foul	hear	meat
bawl	bear	fare	fowl	here	meet

Homophones are a challenge. You have to remember which spelling goes with which definition.

 **Try It!** **The words underlined in the following sentences from "Trapped by the Ice!" are parts of homophone pairs. One homophone and its definition are given. Write a definition for the underlined words based on how they are used in the sentence.**

1. By now, the ice <u>floes</u> were breaking up into smaller and smaller pieces all around the men as they drifted closer to the edge of the polar sea.

   flows: moves in a stream   floes: __Answers will vary.__
   Floes are sheets of floating ice.

2. It was Elephant Island at last. It looked terribly <u>barren</u>, with jagged 3,500-foot peaks rising right up out of the sea . . .

   baron: a nobleman of Europe   barren: __Answers will vary.__
   Land that is barren has little vegetation.

3. Water filled the *Caird* while the men <u>bailed</u> furiously.

   baled: made into a bundle   bailed: __Answers will vary.__
   Bailed means cleared a boat of water.

UNIT 6 Journeys and Quests • **Lesson 2** *Trapped by the Ice!*

Homophones

Practice

Fill in the blank in each sentence with the appropriate homophone.

floes	flows	barren	baron	bailed
baled	whaling	wailing	pier	peer

4. The baby was ____wailing____ because it had lost its pacifier.

5. The desert land was ____barren____ and would only support the growth of a few small shrubs and cacti.

6. The farm hands ____baled____ hay into neat bundles that would be kept in the barn.

7. The sailor would ____peer____ out the porthole at the swelling waves of the sea.

8. People of the nineteenth century would go ____whaling____ and use the fat of these large sea mammals to light their lamps.

9. The rowboat sprang a leak and quickly filled with water, so we ____bailed____ as fast as we could.

10. The Mississippi River ____flows____ south into the Gulf of Mexico.

11. The ____baron____ was a rich and powerful man in Austria.

12. We walked out onto the ____pier____ and found a small boat tied to a post.

13. The ice ____floes____ moved slowly and were hundreds of feet long.

VOCABULARY

Latin Roots

Word List

1. transistor
2. transfer
3. credit
4. record
5. applaud
6. audition
7. hospitality
8. faculty
9. animal
10. captain
11. dentist
12. doctor
13. introduction
14. popular
15. vacuum

Selection Words

16. terrain
17. recognized
18. monstrous
19. miraculous
20. temporary

Pattern Study

Understanding the meanings of Latin roots can help you spell many new words. Here are some of the Latin roots in the spelling words and their meanings.

trans = across	**cred** = believe	**aud** = hear
hosp = host	**anim** = life	**cap** = head
dent = tooth	**doc** = teach	**duc** = lead
pop = people	**vac** = empty	**terr** = land
cogn = know	**cord** = heart	**temp** = time
laud = praise		

▶ Fill in the Latin root and write the whole spelling word.

1. _____ al   **animal** _____
2. _____ uum   **vacuum** _____
3. _____ tain   **captain** _____
4. _____ istor   **transistor** _____
5. app _____   **applaud** _____
6. _____ orary   **temporary** _____
7. _____ ular   **popular** _____
8. _____ fer   **transfer** _____
9. intro _____ tion **introduction** _____
10. _____ it   **credit** _____
11. re _____ ized **recognized** _____
12. _____ ition **audition** _____

UNIT 6 Journeys and Quests • **Lesson 2** *Trapped by the Ice!*

▶ **Latin Roots**

Strategies

Meaning Strategy Write the spelling word that represents each of the following Latin root meanings. Use the Latin roots and meanings on page 140 to help you.

13. praise **applaud**

14. people **popular**

15. land **terrain**

16. time **temporary**

17. hear **audition**

18. lead **introduction**

19. tooth **dentist**

20. believe **credit**

Family Strategy Write the spelling word that contains the same Latin root as each of the following words.

21. hospital **hospitality**

22. dental **dentist**

23. population **popular**

24. incredible **credit**

25. vacant **vacuum**

SPELLING

UNIT 6 Journeys and Quests • **Lesson 3** *Apollo 11: First Moon Landing*

Derivations

> As you learned in Unit 2, many of the words we use in English contain roots that originally came from Greek and Latin. English words are derived, or taken, from words and roots in these older languages. For example, the word *astronomy* is derived from the Greek root ***astr,*** meaning "star."

 **The following words are from the selection "Apollo 11: First Moon Landing." Write each word next to its definition and the Greek or Latin root or word from which it is derived.**

aviation	hydrogen	circumference
tranquility	quarantine	

1. *tranquillus*

the state of being at rest and free of turmoil **tranquility** _____

2. *avis*

the operation of aircraft **aviation** _____

3. *circum + ferre*

the perimeter of a circle **circumference** _____

4. *quadraginta*

the isolation of people suspected of carrying contagious

disease **quarantine** _____

5. *hydr*

a colorless, odorless gas **hydrogen** _____

UNIT 6 Journeys and Quests • **Lesson 3** *Apollo 11: First Moon Landing*

▶ **Derivations**

Practice

The following groups of words were all derived from the same Greek or Latin root. Using what you know about their meanings, write the meaning of each root.

6. donation: a gift
   donor: a person who gives something
   donate: to give

   What does the Latin root *don* mean? **give**

7. location: a place where something is
   locate: to find the place or position of
   dislocate: to put out of a proper or normal position

   What does the Latin root *loc* mean? **place**

8. marine: having to do with the sea
   submarine: a ship that can travel underwater
   marina: a small harbor where boats can be docked

   What does the Latin root *mar* mean? **sea**

9. microscope: a device for looking at tiny things
   telescope: an instrument that helps us see faraway things
   periscope: a device on a submarine used to see above the water

   What does the Greek root *scop* mean? **see**

10. transport: to bring or carry from one place to another
    portable: easy to carry from place to place
    import: to bring in goods from another country

    What does the Latin root *port* mean? **carry**

VOCABULARY

UNIT 6 Journeys and Quests • **Lesson 3** *Apollo 11: First Moon Landing*

Words of Spanish Origin

Word List

1. alfalfa
2. cafeteria
3. banana
4. marina
5. salsa
6. oregano
7. patio
8. lasso
9. silo
10. burrito
11. alligator
12. plaza
13. corral
14. ranch
15. mesa
16. canyon
17. tortilla
18. nacho
19. burro
20. rodeo

Pattern Study

Many words we use in English come from Spanish. A number of these words are food words and words used to describe something in Southwestern or South American culture. Spanish words often end in *o* or *a*.

▶ Write the spelling words that end with the letter *o*.

1. oregano
2. patio
3. lasso
4. silo
5. burrito
6. nacho
7. burro
8. rodeo

▶ Write the spelling words that end with the letter *a*.

9. alfalfa
10. cafeteria
11. banana
12. marina
13. salsa
14. plaza
15. mesa
16. tortilla

▶ Write the spelling words that end in a letter other than *o* or *a*.

17. alligator
18. corral
19. ranch
20. canyon

UNIT 6 Journeys and Quests • **Lesson 3** *Apollo 11: First Moon Landing*

▶ **Words of Spanish Origin**

SPELLING

Strategies

Visualization Strategy Fill in the missing vowels and write the spelling words correctly.

21. pl__z__   **plaza** _____

22. n__ch__   **nacho** _____

23. p__ti__   **patio** _____

24. s__l__   **silo** _____

25. r__de__   **rodeo** _____

26. or__g__n__   **oregano** _____

27. t__rt__ll__   **tortilla** _____

28. m__s__   **mesa** _____

29. c__f__t__ria   **cafeteria** _____

30. m__r__n__   **marina** _____

Meaning Strategy Fill in each blank with the spelling word that best completes the sentence.

31. An ___**alligator**___ is related to a crocodile but is not exactly the same.

32. After a day of grazing in the fields, the horses were herded into the ___**corral**___.

33. The cowboy used a ___**lasso**___ to rope the runaway calf.

34. My grandparents' ___**ranch**___ in New Mexico employs a dozen workers and has thousands of cattle.

35. A ___**burro**___ looks like a donkey and is used to carry heavy loads.

UNIT 6 Journeys and Quests • **Lesson 4** *When Shlemiel Went to Warsaw*

Multicultural Words

As you read stories and other texts about people and events in other countries, you will come across multicultural words from different languages and cultures. Take a look at these Yiddish and German words from "When Shlemiel Went to Warsaw."

cheder: a school for Jewish children that also teaches religious knowledge

blintze: a kind of pancake that is often filled

shlemiel: an awkward or clumsy person

groschen: an amount of money; 100 groschen equal one schilling

elder: an officer in a church or synagogue

 **Now that you know the definitions for these multicultural words from "When Shlemiel Went to Warsaw," fill in each blank with the word that best completes each sentence.**

1. Shlemiel's wife sought the advice of a town ___**elder**___ when her husband did not realize he was home.

2. The children especially like to eat a ___**blintze**___ made by their mother.

3. The bumbling main character in the story lives up to his name, for he is a real ___**shlemiel**___.

4. Shlemiel's children hurried to finish their breakfast so they would not be late for ___**cheder**___.

5. The family was poor, and only had a few ___**groschen**___ to spare.

Multicultural Words

VOCABULARY

Practice

Use each of these vocabulary words from "When Shlemiel Went to Warsaw" in a sentence of your own. Make sure your sentence shows that you know the meaning of the vocabulary word.

6. cheder: **Answers will vary.** _____

_____

_____

7. blintze: **Answers will vary.** _____

_____

_____

8. shlemiel: **Answers will vary.** _____

_____

_____

9. groschen: **Answers will vary.** _____

_____

_____

10. elder: **Answers will vary.** _____

_____

_____

Words of French Origin

Word List

1. crochet
2. balloon
3. detour
4. amateur
5. avalanche
6. ballet
7. baton
8. perfume
9. beret
10. buffet
11. mentor
12. mirage
13. croquet
14. collage
15. café
16. cassette
17. bouquet
18. boulevard
19. blond
20. chef

Pattern Study

Many words we use in English come from French. French words often have different pronunciations than the English words you know. For example, French words frequently contain the /ā/ sound spelled *et*, *ait*, or *e*.

▶ Write the spelling word after its pronunciation.

1. krō shā´ — **crochet**
2. am´ ə tər — **amateur**
3. ba lā´ — **ballet**
4. shef — **chef**
5. ka fā´ — **café**
6. mə räzh´ — **mirage**
7. bō kā´ — **bouquet**
8. av´ ə lanch — **avalanche**
9. bə fā´ — **buffet**
10. bə rā´ — **beret**
11. dē´ to͞or — **detour**
12. kə läzh´ — **collage**
13. krō kā´ — **croquet**
14. bə ton´ — **baton**

UNIT 6 JOURNEYS AND QUESTS • **Lesson 4** *When Shlemiel Went to Warsaw*

▶ **Words of French Origin**

SPELLING

Strategies

Proofreading Strategy Circle the misspelled word in each of the following sentences and write it correctly on the line that follows.

15. We put the video (casette) into the recorder to tape our
favorite sitcom. **cassette**

16. The boy let go of his (baloon) and watched with
disappointment as it floated up into the sky. **balloon**

17. She looked up to her teacher as a (mentour) and a friend. **mentor**

18. Only three of the girls in our class have (blound) hair. **blond**

19. My aunt and uncle live on a shady (boulavard) with lots of
trees. **boulevard**

Visualization Strategy Choose the correct spelling for each word and write it on the following lines.

20.	shef	chef	cheff	**chef**
21.	ballet	ballay	balle	**ballet**
22.	crokay	croket	croquet	**croquet**
23.	mirage	merage	mirrorage	**mirage**
24.	buffe	boufet	buffet	**buffet**
25.	amatuer	amature	amateur	**amateur**
26.	bouquet	bokay	boquet	**bouquet**
27.	avalanch	avalanche	avelanche	**avalanche**
28.	perfum	purfume	perfume	**perfume**

UNIT 6 Journeys and Quests • **Lesson 5** *The Search*

Metaphor

A metaphor is a creative and original comparison between two things that are not normally compared. A metaphor, however, does not contain *like* or *as*. It states that one thing **is** another thing. Here are some examples:

▶ My book is a spaceship that helps me travel across galaxies.

▶ The mist was a heavy blanket spread over the valley.

The following sentences are examples of metaphors. Study the metaphors carefully. Then write a definition for the underlined words based on context clues.

1. In an emergency, he is a strong and steady <u>juniper</u> standing tall in the forest.

   juniper: **an evergreen tree** _____

2. The multiplication problem was a <u>chaparral</u>, a dense group of shrubs and trees that I could not see through.

   chaparral: **a dense thicket of trees and shrubs** _____

3. Her cranky personality was a prickly <u>peyote</u> in the desert.

   peyote: **a cactus** _____

4. The kind mother was a gentle <u>ewe</u> watching over her lambs.

   ewe: **a female sheep** _____

5. While I daydreamed, lazy thoughts went <u>ambling</u> through my brain, as if they were on a leisurely walk.

   ambling: **walking at a leisurely pace** _____

Practice

Below are examples of simile and metaphor. Put an X next to the metaphors.

6. When she finished her test, she was as happy as a lark.

_____

7. The ice cream was frozen as hard as a rock. _____

8. We tried to persuade her to join the basketball game, but

she was a stubborn mule. **X** _____

9. He cried like a baby when he thought he was lost in the

department store. _____

10. The dewdrops were diamonds glistening on the lawn.

X _____

UNIT 6 Journeys and Quests • **Lesson 5** *The Search*

Other Foreign Words

Word List

1. bagel
2. ballerina
3. gusto
4. khaki
5. macaroni
6. mascara
7. parka
8. safari
9. sauna
10. tycoon
11. veranda
12. yogurt
13. karate
14. boomerang
15. pasta
16. pepperoni
17. polka
18. ravioli
19. pizza
20. opera

Pattern Study

Words from Italian, German, Japanese, Yiddish, Hindi, Turkish, Finnish, Kiswahili, and even the language of the native Australians are used in English. Many of the spelling words are Italian. Italian words are often food or music words and frequently end in *o*, *a*, or *i*.

▶ Write each spelling word after its origin and definition.

1. *Turkish:* a creamy food made of milk and cultures of bacteria **yogurt**

2. *Kiswahili:* a hunting trip in Africa **safari**

3. *Italian:* a story or play set to music **opera**

4. *German:* a lively dance **polka**

5. *Aboriginal:* a club that is bent so that it returns when thrown **boomerang**

6. *Japanese:* an art of self defense involving kicks and punches **karate**

7. *Aleutian:* a hooded coat often worn in very cold lands **parka**

8. *Finnish:* a steam bath made by pouring water over hot stones **sauna**

UNIT 6 Journeys and Quests • **Lesson 5** *The Search*

► **Other Foreign Words**

Strategies

Meaning Strategy **Fill in each blank with the spelling word that best completes the sentence.**

9. He cut the _____**bagel**_____ in half, toasted it in the toaster, and spread cream cheese on it.

10. My sister is a _____**ballerina**_____ and needs new toe shoes before she can perform in *The Nutcracker*.

11. We couldn't decide if we wanted pepperoni or sausage on our _____**pizza**_____, or if we wanted a small, medium, or large size.

12. It is a good idea to wear a _____**parka**_____ when you go to Alaska to shield yourself from the snow and cold.

13. We danced the _____**polka**_____ at our cousin's wedding.

Proofreading Strategy **Circle the misspelled word in each of the following sentences and write it correctly.**

14. Charles is taking classes in (karati) and has already earned his brown belt. _____**karate**_____

15. I like my (yogert) flavored with fruit, such as strawberries and blueberries. _____**yogurt**_____

16. Marie has a (boomarang) that always sails back to her after she throws it into the air. _____**boomerang**_____

17. The restaurant offers (raviolli) that is stuffed with cheese, spinach, or ground beef. _____**ravioli**_____

18. We were starving and ate our bowls of pasta with (gusto). _____**gusto**_____

SPELLING

UNIT 6 Journeys and Quests • **Lesson 6** *Alberic the Wise*

▶ Review

> Remember that the words we use in English have their roots in many other languages. English words can contain Greek or Latin roots, such as *geo* and *luc,* that give us clues about their meanings. English words can come from many other languages and cultures, such as French, Spanish, German, Italian, Yiddish, and Japanese. As you discover words from other languages and cultures, try to learn their meanings.

 Write the following words from the selection "Alberic the Wise" next to their origins and definitions.

cloister	pungent	tunic	embellished	bastion

1. Latin, *tunica:* a simple, sleeveless garment that is at least knee-length and belted at the waist ___**tunic**___

2. French, *bastille:* a projecting part of a fort ___**bastion**___

3. French, *embeliss:* decorated ___**embellished**___

4. Latin, *claudere:* a covered walkway on the side of a courtyard ___**cloister**___

5. Latin, *pugnus:* having a sharp odor ___**pungent**___

UNIT 6 Journeys and Quests • **Lesson 6** *Alberic the Wise*

▶ **Review**

Practice

Now that you have discovered the meanings of the vocabulary words from "Alberic the Wise," use each word in a sentence of your own.

6. cloister: Answers will vary. _____

_____

_____

7. pungent: Answers will vary. _____

_____

_____

8. tunic: Answers will vary. _____

_____

_____

9. embellished: Answers will vary. _____

_____

_____

10. bastion: Answers will vary. _____

_____

_____

VOCABULARY

UNIT 6 Journeys and Quests • **Lesson 6** *Alberic the Wise*

▶ Review

Word List

1. restaurant
2. barrette
3. royalty
4. ambulance
5. computer
6. thermos
7. hydrant
8. police
9. podium
10. coyote
11. poncho
12. llama
13. original
14. casserole
15. spaghetti

Selection Words

16. beautiful
17. optimism
18. solitary
19. instruction
20. remember

Pattern Study

As you read, you will be able to recognize and spell more words with Greek and Latin roots, and words that come from foreign languages such as Spanish, French, and Italian.

▶ Fill in the missing letters and write the spelling words on the lines below.

1. s__l__tary
   solitary

2. p__nch__
   poncho

3. h__dr__nt
   hydrant

4. b____tiful
   beautiful

5. c____ote
   coyote

6. amb__l__nce
   ambulance

7. pol____e
   police

8. cass__r__l__
   casserole

9. bar__et____
   barrette

10. spag__e____i
    spaghetti

11. th__rm__s
    thermos

12. or__g__n__l
    original

13. rest____r__nt
    restaurant

14. instr__c__ion
    instruction

Review • Spelling and Vocabulary Skills

UNIT 6 Journeys and Quests • **Lesson 6** *Alberic the Wise*

► **Review**

SPELLING

Strategies

Visualization Strategy Fill in the Greek or Latin root and write the complete spelling word.

15. _ _ _ _ _ _ance

ambulance
_____

16. com_ _ _er

computer
_____

17. _ _ _ _ _ _os

thermos
_____

18. _ _ _ _ant

hydrant
_____

19. _ _ _imism

optimism
_____

20. _ _ _ium

podium
_____

21. _ _ _ _inal

original
_____

22. re_ _ _ber

remember
_____

23. _ _ _itary

solitary
_____

Meaning Strategy Write the correct spelling word for each definition.

24. An animal related to the camel, but without a hump

llama
_____

25. Persons of royal rank **royalty**
_____

26. A clip that holds the hair in place **barrette**
_____

27. A North American animal related to the wolf

coyote
_____

28. A cloak that looks like a blanket **poncho**
_____

Vocabulary Rules

Synonyms are words that are similar in meaning.

> The solution to the puzzle is **easy.**
> The solution to the puzzle is **simple.**

Antonyms are words that are opposite in meaning.

> An elephant is a **large** animal.
> A mouse is a **small** animal.

Homophones are words that are pronounced alike but are spelled differently and have different meanings.

> The wind **blew** white clouds across the **blue** sky.

Some common homophones are **their/there/they're; your/you're;** and **it's/its.**

- *Their* means "belonging to them." *There* means "in that place," or it may be used at the beginning of a sentence with *is, are, was,* or *were. They're* is a contraction for "they are."

  They're happy that **their** team won over **there.**

- *Your* is a possessive pronoun meaning "belonging to you." *You're* is a contraction for "you are."

  You're sure **your** team won?

- *Its* is a possessive pronoun meaning "belonging to it." *It's* is a contraction for "it is."

  It's a shame that the tree lost **its** leaves so soon.

Context Clues

When you come to a new word in your reading, you can sometimes figure out the meaning of the word from its context, the words and sentences around it. Writers give context clues in five main ways.

▶**Definition** The meaning of the word is stated.

>Mother ordered a *cushion*, which is a **soft pillow.**

▶**Example** The meaning of the unfamiliar word is explained through examples.

>Her *interjections*—**Ouch! Wow!**—are so dramatic.

▶**Comparison** The unfamiliar word is similar to a familiar word or phrase.

>Why would I *retract* my statement? I will not **withdraw** it.

▶**Contrast** The unfamiliar word is opposite a familiar word or phrase.

>She is really a *novice*, although she appears **experienced.**

▶**Cause and Effect** The unfamiliar word is explained as part of a cause-and-effect relationship.

>He really enjoyed the *hors d'oeuvres* tonight because he always has a **snack** before dinner.

Multiple-Meaning Words

Multiple-meaning words are words that have the same spelling and pronunciation but have more than one meaning and may be different parts of speech in different situations.

> **gorge**
> Noun: **a deep, narrow valley with steep sides**
> Verb: **to eat greedily**

Word Roots

A word root is the main part of a word. Sometimes a prefix or suffix is added to it. These additions often change a word's meaning or its part of speech.

> **Audio** means "hear."
>
> An **audiotape** is a tape you **listen** to.
> An **audience** is a group that **hears** a performance.
> **Audiovisual** materials help us see and **hear** what we are learning.

Prefixes and Suffixes

- **Prefixes** are word parts added to the beginning of a root to change its meaning.

  > A **co**worker is a person with whom one works.
  > To **co**write is to write together.

- **Suffixes** are word parts added to the end of a root to change its meaning.

  > Fear**ful** means "full of fear."
  > A spoon**ful** is the amount that fills a spoon.

Spelling Strategies

There are many different ways to learn how to spell. A spelling strategy is a plan that can make learning to spell easier. Take some time to learn how these strategies can help you spell better.

Sound Pattern Strategies

Pronunciation Strategy
Learn to listen to the sounds in a word. Then spell each sound. *(sit)*

Consonant-Substitution Strategy
Try switching consonant letters without changing the vowel. *(bat, hat, rat, flat, splat) / (mat, mad, map, mask)*

Vowel-Substitution Strategy
Try switching the vowel letters without changing the rest of the word. *(hit, hat, hut, hot) / (mane, mine) / (boat, beat)*

Rhyming Strategy
Think of a word that rhymes with the spelling word and has the same spelling pattern. *(cub, tub, rub)*

Structural Pattern Strategies

Conventions Strategy
Think about the rules and exceptions you have learned for adding endings to words. *(crying, cried)*

Visualization Strategy
Think about how the word looks. Most words look wrong when they do not have the right spelling. *(can, not cen)*

Proofreading Strategy
Check your writing carefully for spelling mistakes.

Meaning Pattern Strategies

Family Strategy
Think of how words from the same family are spelled. *(art, artist)*

Meaning Strategy
Think about the meaning of the word to make sure you're using the right word. *(see, sea)*

Compound Word Strategy
Break the compound into its two words to spell each word. *(homework, home work)*

Foreign Language Strategy
Think of foreign word spellings that are different from English spelling patterns. *(ballet)*

Dictionary Strategy
Find the word in a dictionary to make sure your spelling is correct.

Spelling Rules

General Spelling Rules for Most Words

- All words have at least one vowel.
- Most words have at least one consonant.
- Every syllable has a vowel or the letter *y*.
- Many words are spelled exactly as they sound.
- Some words are exceptions to spelling rules and must be memorized.

Consonant Spellings

Most consonants sound like their letter names.

- /b/ is spelled *b* as in *bad*
- /d/ is spelled *d* as in *dash*
- /f/ is spelled *f* as in *fast*
- /j/ is spelled *j* as in *jog*
- /k/ is spelled *k* as in *kiss*
- /l/ is spelled *l* as in *lot*
- /m/ is spelled *m* as in *map*

- /n/ is spelled *n* as in *nest*
- /p/ is spelled *p* as in *pin*
- /r/ is spelled *r* as in *rug*
- /s/ is spelled *s* as in *sand*
- /t/ is spelled *t* as in *tip*
- /v/ is spelled *v* as in *vat*
- /z/ is spelled *z* as in *zip*

Some consonants do not sound like their letter names.

- /h/ does not sound like the letter *h*. *(hill)*

- /w/ does not sound like the letter *w*. *(wish)*

- /y/ does not sound like the letter *y*. *(yell)*

- There are hard and soft sounds for the letter *c*.
    hard *c*: /k/ is spelled *c* as in *can*
    soft *c*: /s/ is spelled *c* as in *cell*

- There are hard and soft sounds for the letter *g*.
    hard *g*: /g/ is spelled *g* as in *gum*
    soft *g*: /j/ is spelled *g* as in *gym*

Consonant Blends

Consonant blends are two- or three-letter combinations in which each letter can be heard.

- Three main groupings are the *s*-blends, *r*-blends, and *l*-blends.

- Two-letter *s*-blend /sl/ is spelled *sl* as in *slip*
  /sp/ is spelled *sp* as in *speak*
  /sk/ is spelled *sk* as in *sky*
  /sk/ is spelled *sc* as in *scare*
  /sm/ is spelled *sm* as in *smell*
  /sn/ is spelled *sn* as in *snow*
  /st/ is spelled *st* as in *stack*
  /sw/ is spelled *sw* as in *swim*

- The blends *sc* and *sk* both spell the /sk/ sound. *(scan, skip)*

- When you hear the /sk/ sound at the end of a word, spell it *sk*, not *sc*. *(risk, not risc)*

- Only a few words have *sp* at the end, such as *wasp* and *lisp*.

- Three-letter *s*-blend /skr/ is spelled *scr* as in *scream*
  /spl/ is spelled *spl* as in *split*
  /spr/ is spelled *spr* as in *spray*
  /str/ is spelled *str* as in *string*

- Blends found at the ends of words:
  /ft/ is spelled *ft* as in *gift*   /ld/ is spelled *ld* as in *bald*
  /lf/ is spelled *lf* as in *elf*   /lk/ is spelled *lk* as in *milk*
  /lp/ is spelled *lp* as in *help*   /lt/ is spelled *lt* as in *wilt*

- The *l* is silent in *half* and *calf*.

- The final-consonant blends *mp*, *nd*, *ng*, *nk*, and *nt* are found at the end of one-syllable words. Most often, the vowel that comes before the blend has a short-vowel sound.

Consonant Digraphs are the letter combinations *ch, qu, th, wh, sh, ph,* and *gh* that stand for a single sound.

- *qu, wh,* and *ph* are usually found at the beginning of a word.
- The letter *u* almost always follows the letter *q,* as in *quick.*
- *th* can be "voiced" as in *then* or "unvoiced" as in *thank.*
- Some words, like *shred,* combine three consonants to form a consonant blend.

Consonant Choices

- The most common spelling for the /s/ sound is *s,* as in *simmer.* Other spellings are *ss, se,* and *ce,* as in *cross, once,* and *horse.* When the /s/ sound is followed by the letters *i, e,* or *y,* it is often spelled *c* or *sc,* as in *city* or *science.*
- The /k/ sound can be spelled *c* or *k* at the beginning of words such as *kite* and *cake.* A few words have the /k/ sound spelled *ch,* as in *chorus.* The /k/ sound spelled *ck* is found at the end of a word, as in *back.*
- The /j/ sound is usually spelled *j* as in *joke.* At the end of some words, such as *fudge* and *huge,* /j/ can be spelled *dge* or *ge.* Before the letters *e, y,* or *i,* the /j/ sound can be spelled *g,* as in *giant, gem,* or *gym.*

Double-Consonant Spellings

- Most double-consonant patterns occur in the middle or final position of a word, as in *stall, pizza,* and *lettuce.*
- The most common double consonants in the final position are *ff, ss,* and *ll,* as in *cliff, cross,* and *still.*
- Double consonants are rarely found at the beginning of a word, as in *llama* and *Lloyd.*

Silent Letters

- *g* is silent in the letter combination *gn* at the beginning or end of a word such as *gnome* or *sign.*
- *k* is silent in the letter combination *kn* at the beginning of a word such as *knight.*
- *b* is silent in the letter combination *mb* at the end of a word such as *thumb.*
- *w* is silent in the letter combination *wr* at the beginning of a word such as *write.*
- The *g* is not silent in a word in which *gn* is divided into syllables, as in *signal.*
- Some words have *mb* followed by *le,* in which the *b* is not silent, as in *thimble, tumble,* and *crumble.*

SHORT-VOWEL SOUND SPELLINGS

Short-vowel sound spellings are more predictable than long-vowel sound spellings.

- Short-vowel sounds most often are found in words beginning with a vowel, such as *up*, *at*, and *end*, or words with *vowel-consonant* or *vowel-consonant-consonant* endings, such as *cup*, *bat*, and *lend*.
- Some short-vowel sounds are spelled with two or more letters, such as *bread* and *laugh*.
- Short vowels have many simple spelling patterns, such as *at*, *in*, *ot*, *et*, and *ug*.

The /a/ Sound

- /a/ is spelled *a*, as in *cat*.
- /a/ can also be spelled *a_e*, as in *have*.

The /e/ Sound

- /e/ is most often spelled *e*, as in *bed*.
- /e/ can be spelled _*ea*_ in the middle of a word, as in *bread* or *head*.

The /i/ Sound

- /i/ is most often spelled *i*, as in *did*.
- When *y* is found in the middle of a word, it acts like a vowel. It usually makes the /i/ sound, as in *system*.
- /i/ is sometimes spelled *i_e*, as in the words *give* and *live*.

The /o/ Sound

- /o/ is usually spelled *o*, as in *got*.

The /u/ Sound

- /u/ is usually spelled *u*, as in *fun*.
- /u/ can be spelled *o*, as in *son*, or *o_e*, as in *glove* and *love*.

The /oi/ Sound

- /oi/ is spelled _*oy* or *oi*, as in *boy*, *boil*, and *oil*.
- The *oi* spelling is found at the beginning and in the middle of words.
- The *oy* spelling is mostly found at the end of a word and sometimes at the end of a syllable, as in *loyal*.

The /oo/ Sound

- /oo/ can be spelled *u* or *oo*, as in *pull* and *book*.
- In a few words, /oo/ can be spelled *ou_*, as in *could*.

LONG-VOWEL SOUND SPELLINGS

Long vowels sound like the letter names.
When long-vowel sounds are spelled with two vowels, the first vowel is usually heard and the second vowel is silent.

Vowel-consonant-e
- Many long-vowel sounds have the common *vowel-consonant-e* spelling pattern in which the *e* is silent, as in the word *date*.

The /ā/ Sound
- /ā/ is spelled *a, a_e, ai_,* and *_ay,* as in *agent, base, raid,* and *today.* The *ay* spelling is found at the end of words, and the *ai* spelling is found in the middle of words.

The /ē/ Sound
- /ē/ is often spelled *e, e_e, ee, ea,* and *_y* at the end of words such as *be, here, agree, easy,* and *happy.*
- /ē/ is spelled *ei* in a few words such as *receive,* but also *ie* as in *pierce.* Remember the rhyme: "Write *i* before *e,* except after *c,* or when it sounds like /ā/ as in *neighbor* and *weigh.*"

The /ī/ Sound
- /ī/ is spelled *i, i_e, igh,* and *_y,* as in *icy, site, high,* and *dry.*

The /ō/ Sound
- /ō/ is spelled *o, o_e, oa_,* and *_ow,* as in *pony, bone, boat,* and *snow.*

The /ū/ Sound
- /ū/ is spelled *u, _ue* or *u_e,* as in *unit, cue,* and *cube.*

The /o͞o/ Sound
- /o͞o/ can be spelled *oo* in the middle of a word such as *tool,* *u* in the *u_e* pattern as in *tune,* or *_ew* at the end of a word such as *new.*

THE SCHWA SOUND

Unaccented syllables have a vowel sound called a schwa that is represented by a vowel. A variety of vowels can stand for the schwa sound. Visualizing how a word should look or over-pronouncing the ending as you spell it may help.

Schwa *-ant, -ent, -ance, -ence*
- The endings *-ant* and *-ent* add the meaning "one who" to a word.
- The endings *-ance* and *-ence* add the meaning "state or quality of" to a word.
- More words end in *-ent* and *-ence* than in *-ant* and *-ance*.
- Visualizing how the word should look can help you learn to spell words with these endings.

The /sh/ sound spelled *ti, ci, si*
- Drop the silent *e* before adding the ending.   *race, racial*
- Words that end in *c* or *ce* have the *ci* pattern.   *finance, financial*
- Words that end in *s* usually contain the *si* pattern.   *impress, impression*
- Words that end in *t* often have the *ti* pattern.   *reject, rejection*
- Some words have consonant spelling changes before the endings are added, such as *emit* and *emission*.

Schwa *-el, -al, -le, -il, -ile*
- Most of the time, the /əl/ sound at the end of a word   *little, circle,*
  is spelled *-le*.
- Verbs and action words that end with the /əl/ sound   *dazzle*
  have the *-le* spelling.
- Words that have the *-al* spelling for the /əl/ sound are   *animal, petal*
  usually nouns or adjectives, words that describe nouns.   *final, signal*
- Usually, words that end with the /əl/ sound   *agile, fertile*
  spelled *-ile* are adjectives.
- Words with final syllables that have the /əl/ sound   *towel, label*
  can also be spelled *-el* or *-il*. Usually, these   *gerbil, pencil*
  words are nouns.
- In a few words, the /əl/ final syllable is spelled *-ol*.   *capitol*

STRUCTURAL SPELLING PATTERNS

Plurals
- Add -*s* to most nouns to make them plural. *(cat + s = cats)*
- Add -*es* to words that end in *ch*, *sh*, *s*, *ss*, *x*, *z*, or *zz*.
- Noticing the syllables in the singular and plural forms of a word can help you know whether to add -*s* or -*es*. When -*es* is added, it usually adds another syllable.

Irregular Plurals
- For words that end in *f* or *fe*, change the *f* to a *v* and add -*es*.
- Some plurals are spelled the same as the singular form, such as *deer*.
- The spelling changes in the plural form of some words, such as *tooth* and *teeth*.
- For a word that ends in *consonant-o*, add -*es*. If a word ends in *vowel-o*, -*s* is usually added.

Adding -*ed* and -*ing*
- The ending -*ed* is added to most words to show an action that happened in the past.
- The ending -*ing* is added to a word to show an action that is happening in the present.
- Drop the silent *e* before adding -*ed* and -*ing* to words.

Adding -*er* and -*est*
- The endings -*er* and -*est* are added to words to show comparisons, such as *whiter* and *whitest*.
- Drop the silent *e* before adding these endings to words.

Doubling Final Consonants
- Use the "1-1-1 Check" to double a final consonant:
  1. Does the word have 1 syllable?   *fun*
  2. Does the word have 1 vowel?   *fun*
  3. Does the word end with 1 consonant?   *fun*
     Double the final consonant if all the answers are *yes*. *funny*
- Double the final consonant if the last syllable of the word is accented or stressed.
- Do not double the final consonant if the last syllable is unstressed.
- Do not double the final consonant for words ending in a short vowel and *x*.

MEANING PATTERNS

Word Families *-ous*
- Words that end in *-ous* are common.
- If a word ends in *e*, drop the *e* before adding *-ous*.
- Change *y* to *i* before adding *-ous* to a word that ends in *y*.
- *-ous* added to a word creates an adjective.
- There are a few words with the soft *g* sound, as in *courageous*, in which the final *e* is not dropped.

Vowel-Sound Changes
- When the vowel sound in a base word changes because of an added ending, think of the base-word spelling and use the same vowel that is in the base word. *(major, majority)*

Contractions
- A contraction is a word formed from two or more words. When the words are joined together, some letters are taken out, and an apostrophe (') marks the place.
- Only one letter is taken out of some contractions.

  I am – a = I'm
- Many letters are taken out of some contractions.

  I would – woul = I'd
- The first word in the pair that makes a contraction usually keeps all of its letters.
- Entire words are left out of some contractions.
  (of the clock – f and the = o'clock)
- Some contractions are homophones. *(I'll, aisle; he'd, heed)*
- Make sure you put the apostrophe (') in the right place.
- Leaving out the apostrophe can result in a different word. The word *I'll* becomes the word *ill*.
- Only one contraction, *I'm*, is made with the word *am*.
- Only one contraction, *let's*, is made with the word *us*.
- Some contractions look the same, but mean two different things. *He'd* means "he would" and "he had."
- One contraction, *will not*, changes the spelling and the sound of the omitted letters to become *won't*.

Compound Words

- Compound words are made up of two smaller, complete words. None of the letters are taken out of the words. The spelling of each word stays the same. For example, *news* and *paper* combine to form the compound word *newspaper*.

German and French Spelling Patterns

- Many German words can be recognized by the /ur/ sound spelled -*er* or -*ur*.

    hamb<u>er</u>ger   frankf<u>ur</u>ter

- Some German words end with the /əl/ sound spelled -*el* or have the /ow/ sound spelled *au* or *ow*.

    s<u>au</u>erkraut   pretz<u>el</u>   ch<u>ow</u>der

- Many French words can be recognized by the /ā/ sound spelled *é*, *ée*, *et*, and *ai*. The *t* is silent in *et*.

    entr<u>ée</u>   gourm<u>et</u>   mayonn<u>ai</u>se   caf<u>é</u>

- German words often stress the root syllable.
    French words often stress the final syllable.
    German: hamster   (ham´•ster)
    French: ballet   (bal•let´)

Italian and Spanish Spelling Patterns

- Many Italian and Spanish words end with a vowel.
    Italian: lasagn<u>a</u>   Spanish: avocad<u>o</u>

- Some Italian and Spanish words contain double consonants.
    Italian: pi<u>zz</u>a   Spanish: bu<u>rr</u>o

- The double consonant *ll* in some Spanish words makes the /y/ sound, not the /l/ sound.
    torti<u>ll</u>a

Latin Spelling Patterns

- Latin roots are meaningful word parts that combine with words.

Root	Meaning
scribe, script	to write
form	a shape
sent, sens	to feel
rupt	to break
equa, equi	even
min	to make smaller
mit	to send
bene, beni	well
aud	to hear
port	to carry
dic, dict	to speak
gram	to write

- Some Latin patterns sound like others, which can make them tricky to spell.

Greek Spelling Patterns

- Understanding Greek word patterns and their meanings can help you spell many new words.

Root	Meaning
geo	earth
tele	far off
phon, phone	sounds
hydro	water
micro	small
aster, astr	star
centr	center
phobia	fear
graph	to write
bi, bio	life
cycl	circle
phys	nature
photo	light

- Many Greek roots spell the /f/ sound with the letters *ph*. When you hear the /f/ sound in an unfamiliar word with a Greek root, spell it with a *ph*.